Roadmap to Success

By Laurie Sorensen

Published by Hundredfold Harvest
Harlan, IA

Hundredfold Harvest
653 Oak Road
Harlan, IA 51537-6607

ISBN 978-0-578-85796-1

Printed in the United States of America, the United Kingdom, Australia, and China

TABLE OF CONTENTS

Our Four Plans Process

Lifetime

Two focal points—long view:
- Impact
- Tactical

Annual

One year slice of the legacy plans—what are the things I need to do this year to move toward my desired legacy?

Quarterly

The QPD is quarterly reporting around financial progress, goal completion, general updates, and areas where help is needed. Quarterly goals should flow directly from the three annual plans (Life, Leadership, Business).

Daily

- Choose to do the next thing
- Remember, plans don't self-execute
- Seek progress, not perfection

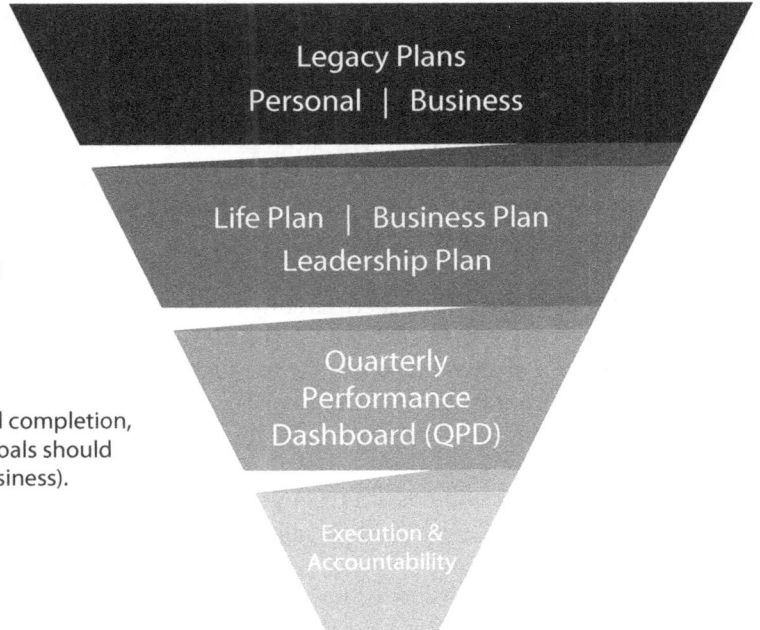

Legacy Plans
Personal | Business

Life Plan | Business Plan
Leadership Plan

Quarterly
Performance
Dashboard (QPD)

Execution &
Accountability

Your Success

If you are interested in using a Quarterly Performance Dashboard
to track and update your performance, download the form at
www.hundrefold-harvest.com/resources

PREFACE

This workbook is designed to guide individuals and teams through implementing the Four Plans. It focuses equally on business and life which distinguishes this from most other planning models.

Updated with our latest thinking around the Four Plans, with legacy as the keystone, this edition of *Roadmap to Success* provides even more resources and examples.

I owe a great debt of gratitude to many. First to my family for their support of this project. Then to Pete Sorensen and Andre Gilmore for their commitment to helping people grow through planning, Scott Scrogin for his repeated help searching for just the right wording to convey an idea, Israel Lang for his generous sharing of ideas and feedback, and Whitney Pearce for her beautiful graphic design and layout of the book.

To our team of talented facilitators, thank you for embracing the Four Plans as one of the pillars of the peer group program and frequently pointing conversations in your room back to members' plans and their desired legacies. Thank you for the tireless and selfless commitment you display to helping your members achieve their individual goals.

I am thankful to our clients, many of whom invite me into their individual journeys with questions about how to make their plans not just a piece of paper but a system that underpins their days. I learn so much from our discussions and gain so much joy from celebrating with you over your wins, big and small. Thank you for your courage in being willing to dream and write down your legacy visions and for your faithfulness in walking toward them.

Lives and businesses are changing for the better as people plan and live their days according to what truly matters. That is our dearest hope for each person who reads this book.

May *Roadmap to Success* ignite success in your life and business as you determine the legacy you desire to build and begin living with that end in mind.

May you plan and live in such a way that your life and leadership outlast you as you intentionally steward your moments for the benefit of others.

Blessings and such JOY as you begin your planning journey,

Laurie Sorensen

FOREWARD

Drift. The enemy of what is best is often what is convenient or even what is good. The reality is that many companies and people fail to achieve what is needed, let alone what they dream of accomplishing.

We see examples of this in our businesses, our leadership, our homes, and, if we are honest, in the person we have a conversation with each morning in the mirror. We wonder why our success seems arbitrary and progress random. Consistency is a mirage.

Yet there are pockets of people all over the globe who are finding a key to success and making consistent progress. Some of the people we work with are seeing their lives and businesses transformed.

Why such a difference? They have discovered the power of legacy. As they shift their mindsets to view everything through the lens of beginning with the end in mind, they envision the legacy they desire, and then they walk toward it by planning and living intentionally.

I wish every person we work with understood the value of legacy. Unfortunately, they are not all there yet, but there are patches of people who do, and I am enjoying watching the ways they are growing and changing for the better. As one person sees transformation, they are igniting success for those around them because others desire that same change for themselves and learn from their example. It's the power of peers at its best.

We are now thrilled to be able to bring this planning methodology that has made such a difference for our clients to you. I can testify that it works—my companies and teams used the Four Plans in our businesses and lives.

There is no secret sauce. The path to success is simply paved with a lot of hard work and dedication. That is why this is such an important and helpful book. We break a complicated subject into practical steps.

By understanding the value of legacy and living intentionally, you can begin your own transformation journey. I encourage you to leverage this planning system for your business and life.

This book is powerful. Read it slowly. Work through it thoughtfully. Allow it to help you shift and learn a new mindset about legacy. And most of all, be a Go-Giver and share what you learn with others.

Arlin Sorensen
Partner, Oak Road Consulting

Planning with the Four Plans

Our Four Plans are integral to the rhythms of our meetings. We believe that regular planning with accountability enables consistent execution around thoughtfully considered goals and thus sets leaders on a journey toward success.

Having good intentions or vague hopes for your life and business is not enough. We believe in the power of personal planning and then walking out those plans in community.

In this section, we will introduce you to the Four Plans foundations and take some first steps toward helping you to develop your own Four Plans.

CHAPTER 1 LESSONS

Walking with Leaders

The Four Plans

What Are Core Values?

Discover Your Personal Values

Discover Your Corporate Values

Walking with Leaders

Have you ever dreamt of having a champion? Someone right there WITH you who understood the unique joys and challenges of your life and business? Someone who was FOR you, dedicated to helping you achieve what you desire?

Our team wants to be that champion for leaders. We design everything we do to help you right where you are on your journey.

Ultimately, though, we don't want you to stay there. Our goal is to empower you to move forward until you achieve your desired growth and legacy.

We exist for you. We want to be with you and for you on your journey. However, it's your growth and legacy. We can't define success for you.

If you don't know where you are going, how can we help?

Roadmap to Success is designed to walk with you as you observe where you are currently and envision your desired future both in terms of your life and your business.

It will guide you in determining where you would like to go and then teach you how to put plans in place to take measured, consistent steps toward getting there.

Life **and** business. It's one thing that sets us apart. We realize that, as humans, we are integrated people. We can't separate our life from our business. The leaders among us who tend toward workaholism to the exclusion of their health or families sometimes need the gentle reminder that "if you are winning at business but failing at life, you are still failing."

Our team doesn't want you to fail. We want you to succeed. In fact, we are audacious enough that we want you to not only succeed but to achieve in-your-wildest-dreams, over-the-top success. We want you to realize your desired growth and legacy for both your business and your life.

We are *for* you. Thanks for the privilege of walking *with* you.

Alongside for the journey,
Your Hundredfold Harvest Team

The Spark That Ignites Success

Imagine moving from where you are today to where you want to be. Can you describe what that would be like?

As one leader did this exercise, he whispered, "It would change everything." It would be transformative.

The Four Plans are igniting success for leaders. We are seeing their lives and businesses change for the better in small ways that compound over time to result in achieving their goals.

We would like to ignite success for you. But first, you need to understand one thing. It's the one thing that makes everything else about the Four Plans fall into place.

What is that one thing?

Legacy Thinking

We call Legacy Thinking our keystone because it is the spark that ignites success in every other area of life and business.

To define Legacy Thinking, we borrow a phrase from author Stephen Covey. Legacy Thinking is "beginning with the end in mind."

In other words, it is thinking about all of life and business through the lens of legacy. It is viewing today in light of your desired impact tomorrow.

This is the reason we emphasize legacy planning and lead with the legacy plan whenever we teach the Four Plans.

Because we strongly believe that if you know where you want to go, we can help you get there.

APPLICATION: Reflect on a time when you had someone who was with you and for you in some part of your business or life. Who was that person? How was their support helpful to you? How do you feel as you begin this planning journey, knowing that our team is with you and for you?

> *When a man does not know what harbor he's making for, no wind is the right wind.*
>
> *– Seneca*

_____

_____

_____

_____

_____

The Four Plans

Begin this lesson by reading the quote in the sidebar and reflecting on this wisdom about planning.

How to Use This Workbook

This workbook is designed to walk you through developing the following Four Plans: legacy plan, life plan, business plan, and leadership plan. Each section will introduce one of the plans and offer exercises to help you think through each step of developing your own plan. We will provide you with templates for each plan as well as examples from other business owners and individuals. These are available both in this book and online in the Resource Library.

How do you eat an elephant? One bite at a time. We realize that completing the plans can be a daunting task, especially if you are relatively new to goal setting and formal planning. We have tried to break each plan down into bite-sized pieces. Each section is comprised of several lessons, most of which you can complete in under 30 minutes per lesson.

The important thing to keep in mind is that plans are never 'finished.' You will be working on your plans forever. Legacy planning, in particular, is an in-depth process. It takes a significant amount of time to thoughtfully consider and put in place all of the tactical areas involved with legacy planning. So, take a deep breath. Give yourself lots of grace. And just take the next bite.

The Structure of the Four Plans

Turn back to the diagram of the plans in the beginning pages of this workbook. As you examine the diagram, you will likely notice several things. First, you may notice that it resembles a funnel. It shows your consistent efforts funneling through the structure of the Four Plans to result in your success. Another thing you will notice is that there are two legacy plans: business legacy and personal legacy.

We believe strongly that to lead your business well, you first must learn to lead yourself and then to lead others. This involves leading at home as well as at work.

Leaning on the wisdom of peers to optimize your business is important. But it is just one small part of the value the Four Plans offer. We leverage the power of community to help you reach your desired growth and legacy.

This begins with taking the step to define what success looks like for you in each area. Then we walk you through creating plans with goals that allow others to provide accountability as you take steps to make success a reality.

How the Plans Fit Together

The personal legacy plan and business legacy plan are vision documents. These paint a picture of your ideal legacy in each area, answering the questions:

- **PERSONAL LEGACY:** What do I desire the impact of my life to have been when I am no longer living?

- **BUSINESS LEGACY:** What do we desire the impact of our leadership and our company to have been when we are no longer leading it?

The legacy plans outline the desired path but do not contain goals. They cast a vision for what is possible. It is the life plan, business plan, and leadership plan that contain goals.

The life plan, business plan, and leadership plan each detail one-year steps toward the vision outlined in the personal legacy plan and business legacy plan. In the year to come, how will I walk toward legacy in the ways that I live and lead? What will the company do this year to build toward that desired future reality?

Legacy Plan	Life Plan	Leadership Plan	Business Plan

Each of the plans can be summarized with a simple question. Draw a line from the plan in the left column to the question that summarizes that plan.

Legacy Plan	How will you live?
Life Plan	How will you lead?
Leadership Plan	How will the company move forward?
Business Plan	How will your leadership and company impact others?

Necessary Mindset Shifts

Adopting the Four Plans planning model necessitates a couple of mindset shifts.

Planning is perpetual.

Traditional planning systems are designed to run on a time-bound basis. People create a plan outlining goals to be accomplished in a year or a quarter, etc.

The Four Plans model is different. It is a perpetual planning model, with each plan designed to be a living document that is constantly adapting and changing.

Rather than creating an annual plan and rejoicing at its completion when all the outlined goals are completed, the completion of a goal on the Life Plan, Business Plan, or Leadership Plan simply triggers an inquiry.

The achieved goal is removed from the plan and a new goal takes its place, one carefully selected by asking "What is the next step to take toward my legacy or the company's legacy?"

Each time a goal is achieved, a new goal takes its place. The plan is never 'finished,' simply refreshed at each periodic review.

Progress, not perfection.

The second necessary mindset shift centers around how one defines success. When legacy vision is defined, it can become easy to feel overwhelmed.

The ideal has now been captured in print. There is an internal struggle between a desire to see it achieved and a fear that it may not come to pass.

Freedom comes when thinking shifts. Instead of an impossible standard of perfection, grace and realism provide freedom. Progress is held up as the standard, not perfection.

Executive Coach Hardin Byars often asks coaching clients a poignant question to help them when perfection tries to assume its place as a harsh taskmaster. He reminds, "Is today better than yesterday? If so, press on."

In other words, even though the desired destination hasn't been completely attained yet, has progress been made? If so, do the next thing. Continue walking toward that defined vision of what success looks like. Each step gets you closer. You'll get there eventually if you press on and refuse to give up. Having a mindset that applauds progress helps you to persevere.

APPLICATION: Read the definition of the word 'Integrity' provided in the margin of this page. How do those definitions relate to the idea of using planning as a tool to drive intentional execution? What would the third definition have to do with tying personal and business planning together? Spend some time reflecting on these questions.

What Are Core Values?

Begin this lesson by reading the quote in the sidebar and reflecting on this wisdom about planning.

Core values are those three to five values that are at the very heart of a company or of a person; they are those things that define us, the ideals we hold most closely.

Core values are like a compass, constantly identifying the true North of a person's or company's ideals.

In this quote, Gandhi illustrates the idea that we become what we believe and live out what we value. Do you agree or disagree? Explain.

_____

_____

_____

Your beliefs become your thoughts. Your thoughts become your words. Your words become your actions. Your actions become your habits. Your habits become your values. Your values become your destiny.

– Mahatma Gandhi

Personal core values answer the question, "How do I want to act as I move toward my desired legacy?" They are foundational and consistent with one's personal mission.

Look back in the paragraphs above. Check the boxes of those things that are descriptors of core values.

❑ Consistent with one's mission   ❑ Foundational

❑ Give concrete steps toward a goal   ❑ Shape how one acts

Here are some basic principles of core values:

- Core values cannot be determined; they can only be discovered.
- Everyone has core values, but many people are not aware of their core values.
- Core values serve to guide you in making decisions.
- Discovering your core values allows you to align your actions with your most closely held ideals.

Which of the principles of core values was new or surprising to you?

❑ Discovered not determined   ❑ Many people are unaware

❑ Align values and actions   ❑ Guide decision making

❑ None of these are new

Picture the Four Plans as a map that guide and empower you to act and move in a predetermined direction. Core values provide boundaries to guide behavior and prevent you from drifting away from what is most important.

A compass is only effective if it is actively utilized; it does no good to have a compass if it stays in a drawer. To be meaningful, our values must influence the choices we make in our everyday living and in doing business.

APPLICATION: For the remaining lessons in this section, we will get practical. You will complete exercises to discover your core values. First, your personal core values and then the core values of your business or organization. To prepare for the next lesson, please spend some time reflecting and journaling about the following questions:

- *What invigorates me? When do I feel most alive? Perhaps you can pinpoint an experience or season in your life when you felt alive. What was true of that period that made it fulfilling?*

- *What stirs up negative emotions inside of me? This can be an indicator of a 'value' that is being violated.*

- *Are there narratives you hold sacred or teachings that you disagree with? What does this contrast point out about what you may value? For example, many religious teachings and philosophies encourage us to show honor to others and consider their interests before our own. This contrasts with the idea of 'looking out for #1' and pursuing our own interests.*

- *Think of someone you deeply respect. Describe three qualities in this person that you admire.*

_____

_____

_____

_____

_____

Discover Your Personal Values

Begin your study by reviewing the prior lesson where we defined core values. Draw a line from the category to its appropriate picture and then from the picture to its descriptor:

Men acquire a particular quality by constantly acting in a particular way.

– Aristotle

Four Plans

Provide boundaries to guide behavior

Core Values

Ensure that your strategy and execution align with your desired growth and legacy

Personal core values are those values that are at the very heart of a person, the ideals one holds most closely. They are an internal reference point for what we believe is good, right, and important.

A personal core value defines the way a person behaves and chooses to interact with others. They are already true of us and can be seen across the broad story of our lives. They are those values that we live out daily and that cause a violent reaction in us when violated.

Part 1: Identifying Your Core Values

Make a list of adjectives that describe what is most important to you. Write down whatever you think of—don't critique your ideas in this initial stage. If you get stuck, look back at your *Application* section from the prior lesson and read through your answers.

_____   _____

_____   _____

_____   _____

_____   _____

_____   _____

_____   _____

Questions to help you define your core values:

- What does the word mean? (start with a dictionary definition)

- Why is this value important to me?

- How do I express this core value?

- Who are the people in my life who demonstrate or represent this value to me?

- What actions are consistent with this value? (at home, at work, etc.)

- What actions are inconsistent with this value? (at home, at work, etc.)

Provided in the appendix of this book is a list of adjectives as well as cards with values and suggested definitions if you would like to consult them. Feel free to add any additional words that strike you as important to your list.

Now let's look at your list of adjectives:

- Eliminate those that are not enduring or will not be as valid in the future as they are currently.

- Star eight of the values that are most important to you. Keep in mind that this does not mean that you do not value the ones you don't select but simply that some values are more important to you than others.

- Finally, circle the three to five values that most define you. These are your core values.

Part 2: Defining Your Core Values

Personal core values are just that; they're personal. So, it is important to take time to define each one clearly to achieve a shared understanding. Here is one statement that is helpful in thinking through what a value looks like in practice: "If I demonstrate this core value consistently, I will…"

In the margin are some other questions to help you define your core values.

Here is an example showing how someone might define the core value of integrity:

Value: Integrity	
Definition	Doing the right thing, no matter who (if anyone) is watching.
Behaviors	Tell the truth at all times Treat all people with equal value Be ethical in all things

Your turn. Fill in a Values Definition Template for each of your three to five Core Values.

Core Value 1:	
Definition	
Behaviors	

Core Value 2:	
Definition	
Behaviors	

Core Value 3:	
Definition	
Behaviors	

Core Value 4:	
Definition	
Behaviors	

Core Value 5:	
Definition	
Behaviors	

Now that you have defined and listed example behaviors, look for alignment (or possible misalignment) between your core values and your current behavior.

- **At the end of my life, how will I know that I have been successful in living this value?**
- **What will the evidence be that my values and actions were aligned? Be specific.**

Part 3: Sharing and Reflecting on Your Core Values

Your core values are the deeply held beliefs that authentically describe your soul.

– John Maxwell

Share your core values with your family and friends and engage them in sharing their own core values. Perhaps post your core values in a prominent place in your home as a reminder of what is most important.

Reflecting on your core values from time to time is a powerful practice. Here are some questions for self-reflection:

- How am I living these values?

- What is challenging about living these values?

- What support or resources would be helpful to me in practicing these values?

- Which behaviors should I start, stop, continue, and/or change to better aligin myself with these values?

CONTINUE	START	STOP	CHANGE

APPLICATION: Thomas Jefferson, third President of the United States, said, "Whenever you are to do a thing, though it can never be known but to yourself, ask yourself how you would act were all the world looking at you and act accordingly."

Look back at the definition of integrity in the margin of page six. Journal about the meaning of this quote considering that definition and link your reflection to what you have learned about core values.

_____

_____

*Those who would like to go further may consider developing joint core values as a couple or, if you have children, selecting family core values in addition to your personal core values.

Discover Your Corporate Values

Begin your study by reviewing the two prior lessons where we defined core values. Fill in the blanks of the definition:

Core values are those _____ values that are at the very heart of a company; they are those things that we want to _____us, the _____ that we hold most closely.

Corporate core values answer the question, "How will we act as we move toward accomplishing our company vision?" They are foundational. The system of core values that an organization develops promotes ethical business practices.

Business leaders trust employees to act on behalf of the company in ways that are true to this shared set of common ideals and objectives. The more clearly defined an organization's value system, the more likely it will serve as an integral part of company culture and provide guidance to employees as they are making decisions and taking actions on behalf of the business.

Lesson Three gave several word pictures. Check the box of the object used to symbolize core values:

❑ Blue Ribbon   ❑ Anchor   ❑ Compass   ❑ Map

Part 1: Identifying Your Corporate Values

There are multiple ways to discover corporate core values. Some companies have the leadership team engage in exercises to identify core values. Still others do a hybrid process of initially using a subset of the staff to narrow down the possibilities, and then allowing the entire staff to be part of the final selection of the business core values. Here is a methodology for one way to guide your staff through discovering your company's core values:

- Select a subset of the staff for the initial part of this exercise, those five to seven individuals who understand your personal core values as a leader, have high credibility with their peers, and are skilled at their job.

- Take a piece of flipchart paper and title it: Our Company Core Values.

- Begin by writing the three to five core values personally held by the CEO/ business leader and explaining each one to the staff. Remind them that just because they are values held by you personally does not necessarily mean they are those held by the company, but you wanted to make the staff aware of your personal core values and use them to start the discussion.

- Then make a list of adjectives that describe what is most important to you as a company.

- Give each participant five yellow and five red dot stickers. Have them place a

HUNDREDFOLD HARVEST'S

CORE VALUES

Influence

Hospitality

Presence

Honor

Community

yellow dot next to the core values with which they agree most, and a red dot by the values with which they agree least.

- Rewrite the core values with which the group has the highest level of agreement and the lowest level of disagreement on a new piece of chart paper.

Keep in mind that this does not mean that you do not value certain things but simply that some values are more important to you than others.

- Give the team members a chance to explain their thought process behind each value.

- Go through a process of selection. You can repeat the dot exercise used above, vote, or use some other method entirely.

- Narrow the list to five or fewer core values. (This can be done by the team or with the entire staff.)

Part 2: Defining Your Corporate Values

Corporate values are unique to a group, so it is important to take time to define each one clearly to achieve a shared understanding. Excellence may be a value held by two different companies. However, the way it is defined and expressed at each will likely differ. Here is one statement that is helpful in thinking about a definition: "As we demonstrate this core value consistently, we will…"

Below are some other questions to help you consider what your core values mean.

- What does this word mean? (start with a dictionary definition)

- Where did this value come from? (usually a person or an event)

- Why is this value important to us?

- Think of an employee who epitomizes each value. How does _____ currently express this core value?

Use the Values Definition Template to help you draft definitions and example behaviors for each of your three to five core values.

Look back at the prior lesson if you need an example.

Core Value 1:	
Definition	
Behaviors	

Core Value 2:	
Definition	
Behaviors	

Core Value 3:	
Definition	
Behaviors	

Core Value 4:	
Definition	
Behaviors	

Core Value 5:	
Definition	
Behaviors	

Take time as a staff to look for alignment (and misalignment) between your core values and current policies and practices. What will the evidence be that our values and actions were aligned? Be specific.

_____

_____

_____

What is one small action step you could take to bring your individual actions more in line with your company's corporate values?

_____

_____

_____

_____

_____

Which policies and practices should you continue, start, stop, and/or change to better express these values?

CONTINUE	START	STOP

Part 3: Sharing and Reflecting on Your Corporate Values

Publish your core values and share them with the entire staff. Make it a big deal!

Then *use* your core values to examine your policies and procedures and make necessary adjustments to get alignment between what you say and what you do. Hire according to your core values. It is impossible to get someone to 'buy-in' to your core values. You need to find individuals who already hold your values and hire them. A bad fit culturally with a strong skill set is still a bad fit and will end up costing your business in the end.

Finally, *reinforce* your core values. Keep them front and center, always in public view with signs around the office or a public 'values moment' at the beginning of each staff meeting. Celebrate when someone is 'caught' doing something that epitomizes your values.

Mind the Gap! Core values determine the boundary lines within which the company desires to function. They provide guidelines for those acting as a representative of the company to understand how to behave. When you become aware of the values that are most important, you also take on the responsibility to align your actions with those values. The moral conduct of an organization depends greatly on the core values of the top executive. It is vitally important that the business owners and management team align their own behaviors with the values they espouse. When values are consistently modeled by those in leadership, those values strengthen culture and become part of the company's DNA.

APPLICATION: On a scale of 1 to 10 (1 being non-alignment, 10 being perfectly aligned), rate how well your leadership team's current behavior aligns with these values. Using the same scale, rate how well your own personal current behavior aligns with these values.

Leadership Team: *1   2   3   4   5   6   7   8   9   10*

Personal: *1   2   3   4   5   6   7   8   9   10*

Personal Legacy Plan

Records ask, *"What are the details?"*

History asks, *"What was the story?"*

Legacy asks, *"What was the impact of that one life over time?"*

Time passes. Eventually, records will be deleted. History will be distorted. Legacy is lasting because it is passed down through the lives of the people we have touched.

The reality is that everyone leaves a legacy. You are leaving a 24-hour legacy today, as you read this.

The only question is whether your legacy will be intentional or accidental. Will you shape your legacy by making choices about how you live out this day? Or will this one-day slice of your legacy simply be the sum of whatever filled the minutes you were breathing during this 24-hour period?

In this chapter let's slow down and begin to take steps toward leaving an intentional legacy, one built choice-by-choice as you live each day.

CHAPTER 2 LESSONS

A Deeper Understanding

Craft a Personal Mission Statement

Personal Legacy Statement

Transformation Strategies

Erecting Guardrails

Financial Considerations

Legal Considerations

Create Your Personal Legacy Plan

A Deeper Understanding

Begin this lesson by reading the paragraph on the previous page introducing this section and spending some time reflecting on the importance of a legacy plan.

Understanding the Importance of Legacy

The Personal Legacy Plan empowers you to live an intentional life that leaves a positive legacy. It answers the question, "What impact do I want my life to have had when I'm no longer living?"

Three Reasons Personal Legacy Plans Are Important

1. **Creating a personal legacy plan forces us to ask ourselves difficult but important questions.** We each receive only one life; it is a gift. What matters most to me? How do I want to steward my time, talent, and treasure to impact others?

2. **A personal legacy plan serves as a filter for life choices.** When you are unsure if a decision is the correct one, looking at it through the lens of your personal core values and your personal legacy plan often brings clarity. A personal legacy plan helps us to live for the important and not mindlessly drift through our days. It protects us from being distracted by things that seem urgent in the moment but have no lasting value.

3. **We will all die someday.** A personal legacy plan eliminates the regret of missed opportunities. For some, death will come suddenly and unexpectedly. For others, it may not be sudden, but we may not be able to communicate the things we want to share with those we love.

    Working through the personal legacy plan ensures that you have tactically done the necessary things to protect your family. It also provides the opportunity to care for our loved ones well through our preparation for the future.

    The things you wish to communicate to family and friends are also recorded in your plan and will be available for them whenever and however the occasion arises.

    A personal legacy plan prompts us to prepare for our passing and preserve our assets in a way that leaves a financial legacy.

    Take a moment to think about the three reasons why personal legacy plans are important. Which reason struck you as new or important?

    _____

There are two parts to legacy planning: the impact of your life and the tactical guardrails you wisely put in place that prevent unexpected circumstances from robbing you of the opportunity to pass on your legacy in the way you desire.

Understanding Your Place in a Larger Story

You exist amid a larger story. You are not the beginning of your story, and you will not be the end. Family stories are part of both the collective and the individual experience.

It is likely that your parents' and grandparents' lives have impacted you and are part of your story just as your life will be part of the tapestry of your children's stories if you have children.

As you spend time considering the lasting impact you want to make, it is wise to first acknowledge the legacy that was left to you by others.

Resist the impulse to rush through this exercise or to complete it with rose-colored glasses. Tell an honest story of the legacy into which you were born—a whole story that includes both the triumphs and the failures, the pain and the healing that your family has experienced.

Describe your grandparents on both sides of your family. What were they like?

_____

_____

What have you learned from them?

_____

_____

Describe your parents. What are (were) they like?

_____

_____

What have you learned from them?

_____

_____

What traditions, ways of thinking, or mannerisms, etc., have you inherited from family members?

_____

_____

This integrated look at both the joyful and the painful parts provides depth that aids us as we seek to 'own' our stories.

Each of our lives has a place in a larger story, a multi-generational narrative. It is this rich perspective that helps to ground our planning in reality.

> *A good character is the best tombstone. Those who loved you and were helped by you will remember you when forget-me-nots have withered. Carve your name on hearts, not on marble.*
>
> *– Charles Spurgeon*

Understanding the Life Domains

A domain is an area of life in which you live, interact, and have an impact. We talk about five life domains that we have found applicable to most people. These are suggested domains. If you find that one does not apply to you, please feel free to substitute a different domain in its place or use four domains. Other domains you might choose include Financial, Service, etc.

Personal: The personal domain is the domain of self. It includes everything pertaining to you physically, emotionally, and intellectually, including your health and internal world.

Family: The family domain includes your nuclear family such as your spouse, children. For those with close extended families, influential extended family members would be included here. For many, extended family would belong in the community domain.

Career: This domain includes everything pertaining to your work or vocation.

Spiritual: This domain pertains to your care and nurture of your spirit and your relationship to what you believe is sacred, be it God or a higher power. It is the part of our life that in the quiet moments resonates with the thought that "there is more to life than this daily lived experience."

Community: This domain includes our interactions with groups in society at large. These may include friendships, collegial relationships, your church, communities like this one, neighbors, your local community, service organizations, extended family who are more distant in relationship, etc.

APPLICATION: Reflect on each of the five life domains. Using the definitions given above, fill in the chart showing who and what would fall into each of your life domains.

For example, if you are the CEO of PrimeTime IT, under Career you would list CEO of PrimeTime IT. If you are married, have two kids, and are close to your in-laws and siblings, note that under Family.

Life Domain	Defining My Life Domains
Personal	
Family	
Career	
Spiritual	
Community	

Craft a Personal Mission Statement

Begin this lesson by reminding yourself of your core values which you discovered in the first section of the workbook. List them below.

_____

A mission statement focuses around who you want to be in terms of your character as well as what you hope to contribute and achieve. It combines your core values with your unique potential and answers the question, "Why do I exist?" A mission statement is an enduring statement of purpose. Together with your core values and legacy statement, it serves as the foundation of your plans. All of the other aspects of your plans need to align with this foundation to ensure you are heading in the right direction.

A mission statement is like a sandbox. Of all the available areas of beach in which to play and live, it defines a specific area where you will focus. You choose to devote your efforts toward building a life and leaving a contribution in a way that utilizes your unique heart, talents, and personality.

A mission statement is a timeless, one-sentence statement that is clear, concise, and memorable. A personal mission statement often consists of three parts:

- **What** do I want to **do?**

- **Who** was I created to **be?** Whom do I want to **help?**

- **What** is the **result?** What **value** will I provide?

Let's tackle these questions with a short five-part exercise.

Part 1: Reflect. Quickly (spending less than a minute per question) jot down answers to the following questions about who you are. Try to be honest and resist the urge to edit your thoughts. Enjoy this exercise and have some fun as you reflect.

What gives you the greatest joy? (Activities, events, hobbies, projects, people, smells, etc.)

_____

_____

What were your favorite things to do as a child? What do you enjoy doing now?

_____

_____

Which activities make you lose track of time?

_____

_____

> _While it is well enough to leave footprints on the sands of time, it is even more important to make sure they point in a commendable direction._
>
> – James Cabell

To laugh often and much; to win the respect of intelligent people and the affection of children; to earn the appreciation of honest critics and endure the betrayal of false friends; to appreciate beauty; to find the best in others; to leave the world a bit better, whether by a healthy child, a garden patch or a redeemed social condition; to know even one life has breathed better because you lived. This is to have succeeded.

- Ralph Waldo Emerson

What are you naturally good at? _____

_____

What do people ask you for help in doing? _____

_____

If you could get a message across to a large group of people, who would those people be? What would your message be?

_____

_____

What were some of the challenges, difficulties, and hardships you've overcome? How did you do it?

_____

_____

Part 2: Action Words. List some action verbs that you connect with. For example, educate, accomplish, encourage, empower, help, guide, master, motivate, nurture, organize, produce, spread, share, satisfy, teach, write, etc.

_____

_____

Part 3: The 'Who.' What causes do you strongly believe in? _____

_____

Are there things you feel you really should do or change, even though you may have dismissed such thoughts many times? What are they?

_____

_____

Given your talents, passions, and values, how could you use these resources to serve or help? Whom would you serve or help? (Think in terms of the world, your family, your friends, your community, etc.)

_____

_____

List out everything and everyone you think you can help. _____

_____

Part 4: The End Goal. How will the 'who' from part 3 benefit from what you 'do' (the verb or verbs you most resonate with from part 2)?

_____

_____

Part 5: Combine. Combine steps two through four into one sentence, ideally 15 words or fewer. Choose one or two elements from each of the four parts in this exercise. Draft a sentence to answer the questions, "What is your purpose? Why do you exist?"

_____

_____

> *He who has a why to live for can bear any how.*
>
> – Friedrich Nietzsche

Here is an example of a personal mission statement:

I exist to steward what has been given to me in ways that benefit others and make a difference in our world.

After seeing the example, look again at what you wrote above. Revise if you would like and write your new mission statement.

MY MISSION STATEMENT

_____

_____

Take a moment and celebrate! You now have a mission statement.

It is valuable to be able to succinctly communicate your mission to someone else. A fun challenge: Can you summarize your mission statement as a bumper sticker?

_____

APPLICATION: On a scale of 1 to 10 (1 being non-alignment, 10 being perfectly aligned), rate how well your personal mission statement aligns with your core values. Then answer the follow-up question below.

Mission Statement: 1   2   3   4   5   6   7   8   9   10

A gap often exists between 'knowing' and 'doing.' What is one action step you can take to live out your personal mission and vision in accordance with your core values?

_____

_____

Personal Legacy Statement

Begin this lesson by reading the quote in the sidebar. Billy Graham says that one of our primary goals should be preparing for our last day.

On a scale of 1 to 10 (1 being not at all prepared, 10 being well-prepared), rate your own current level of preparation for your last day.

My Preparation:　　1　2　3　4　5　6　7　8　9　10

This lesson may prove to be difficult. In this lesson we will tackle the emotional preparation to leave a personal legacy. In the next two lessons, we will begin the task of the practical preparation of your finances and legal affairs.

No one likes to ponder his/her own mortality, but preparing well so that we can finish well is a gift we give our loved ones.

With the death rate still hovering around 100%, it is one of the great equalizers in life. Rich or poor, wise or unwise, famous or not, we will all die. We have no control over how or when our days on this Earth will be over, but we can be intentional in building something that lives after us.

React to the paragraph above. What emotions are you feeling as we begin this lesson (Fear, frustration at your lack of control, anger, desire to leave well, love for your family and friends, nostalgia as you remember the passing of your own loved ones, regret over wasted time, etc.)?

_____

_____

Your personal legacy is about stewarding your time, talent, and treasure well by living intentionally in ways that will outlast your life.

The personal legacy statement provides the reminder that your legacy is not about you. As we learned earlier in this chapter, your story did not start with you, and it will not end with you. Your personal legacy is about using your influence to make an impact. It is future-focused and others-oriented.

Look back to the lesson titled "Craft a Personal Mission Statement," and copy your personal mission statement below.

Does it still resonate with you? If not, spend some more time with the exercises from that lesson until you have a mission statement that grips your heart with the realization "THIS mission is something I could passionately live out for the next 15-20 years." This is one of the most important parts of the entire planning process, so do not rush through determining your mission statement.

_____

With your personal mission statement fresh in our minds, let's begin to draft your personal legacy statement.

Review the Life Domains you defined in a prior lesson.

Dream a bit and imagine life 20 years from now. Give yourself the grace to picture your life having lived your mission statement out faithfully every single day spanning those 20 years.

In the table below, record one or two sentences for each domain describing what that domain is like. Use present tense, writing from the perspective of what is true 20 years from now. Allow the question under the domain name to serve as a prompt.

Life Domain	**Describe Each Life Domain 20 Years from Now** *If you live your personal mission out in this domain faithfully for the next 20 years…what would happen?*
Personal *Who are you? (Describe your inner world, your emotions, your hobbies, your health, your actions.)*	
Family *Who is your family because you were part of them and lived out your mission?*	
Career *What has happened in your career as you live out your unique mission in the workplace?*	
Spiritual *What is your relationship with God or a higher being like because you pursued what is sacred to you faithfully for 20 years?*	
Community *What has happened in your communities as you were a part of them, living out your mission?*	

Read back over your draft as if it were written as one paragraph and verify that it is written in the present tense.

> *For the growing good of the world is partly dependent on unhistoric acts; and that things are not so ill with you and me as they might have been, is half owing to the number who lived faithfully a hidden life, and rest in unvisited tombs.*
>
> – George Eliot, Middlemarch

Live a life that will help others spiritually, intellectually, physically, financially, and relationally. Live a life that serves as an example of what an exceptional life can look like. Let others lead small lives, but not you. Let others argue over small things, but not you. Let others cry over small hurts, but not you. Let others leave their future in someone else's hands, but not you. Leaving a legacy is like planting a tree. As that seed grows into a tree, it will provide seeds so that future generations can then plant their own.

– Jim Rohn & Chris Widener

Sometimes this exercise is easier with an example. The following example was written imagining someone had lived out this personal mission consistently day-in and day-out across the next 20 years: *I exist to steward what has been given to me in ways that benefit others and make a difference in our world.*

The statement describes the results of that intentional living. It shows who this individual becomes as a person, how his family relationships grow, what happens in his career (or in the case of this CEO, in the company since his career is closely aligned with the growth of the company), how his faith matures, and finally what happens in his communities as he has been involved.

Here is an example of a personal legacy statement:

I am calm and laugh frequently, enjoying each day no matter what fills my hours. I practice my woodworking hobby and run to stay in shape.

My wife knows that I cherish her and has many fond memories of laughter and quality time spent together. We have a marriage of oneness. My kids have a dad who believes in them and who advocates for them to understand and achieve their dreams. They learn the value of hard work because we work together, side by side. My parents feel honored by their son and are aging with dignity.

I intentionally built a career that would provide a solid financial future for my family. My company has invested in me through leadership development training and helping me on my career path. I am grateful and work hard to play my part in helping us reach our shared vision as a team. My career is rewarding. I look forward to going to work each day.

I am continuing to grow in my understanding of my place in the lives of those around me, both those I know and those I do not. I accept some things are out of my control, and that everything happens for a reason. My employees feel secure in their jobs because the company is financially sound. They enjoy coming to work and feel like they are part of something bigger than themselves.

APPLICATION: Read your personal legacy statement one more time through the lens of your personal mission statement and your core values. Does it align? Is it a vision that excites and motivates you about the future? Make any revisions you would like and write your complete personal legacy statement below.

_____

_____

_____

_____

Transformation Strategies

trans·for·ma·tion

/ noun /

Begin your study by reading the definitions of transformation in the margin. Write your own definition of what transformation means.

1 A thorough or dramatic change in form or appearance.

_____

2 A metamorphasis.

Picture transformation strategies as stepping stones between your mission and legacy. They answer the question 'How?' How will this desired impact happen? How will I ignite success in this domain? The best way to understand what a transformation strategy is may be in clarifying what it is not.

3 Change for the better.

Synonyms: renewal, revolution, shift

Transformation strategies are not:

- **Goals.** They are high-level strategies.

- **Lengthy.** They are brief phrases.

- **Set in stone.** These are ideas and suggestions for strategies. You will change these strategies over time to fit your circumstances.

- **Comprehensive.** This initial list may not include all the ways you could or desire to ignite success in a particular domain. You will add to it over time.

Let's look back at our example personal legacy statement and practice coming up with some transformation strategies. I've done the personal domain for you.

Life Domain	Personal Legacy Statement	Transformation Strategies
Personal	*I am calm and laugh frequently, enjoying each day no matter what fills my hours. I practice my woodworking hobby and run to stay in shape.*	• Cultivate discipline of gratitude • Run regularly • Practice woodworking

Your turn. Practice writing transformation strategies for the family domain.

Life Domain	Personal Legacy Statement	Transformation Strategies
Family	*My wife knows that I cherish her and has many fond memories of laughter and quality time spent together. We have a marriage of oneness. My kids have a dad who believes in them and who advocates for them to understand and achieve their dreams. They learn the value of hard work because we work together, side by side. My parents feel honored by their son and are aging with dignity.*	

Now look back at your own personal legacy statement and note transformation strategies for each domain. You can copy your personal legacy statement or just flip back and forth to the page where you wrote your statement.

Life Domain	Personal Legacy Statement	Transformation Strategies
PERSONAL		
FAMILY		
CAREER		
SPIRITUAL		
COMMUNITY		

APPLICATION: As you look over your transformation strategies, which are you most excited to dive into first? Which do you think will make the biggest impact initially?

_____

_____

_____

Erecting Guardrails

Picture yourself driving down the interstate highway. What is the purpose of a guardrail on the side of the highway?

_____

Guardrails protect. They provide guidance and show the path the road follows. They also ensure we don't wander into areas where we shouldn't.

In terms of legacy, guardrails are tactical areas that need to be considered in order to protect the practical aspect of legacy. It is also proactive thinking that frees your family to focus on what is most important at the time of your passing: grieving your loss and celebrating a life well-lived.

There are many tactical areas that one could consider when planning for legacy. In this lesson, we will introduce the 11 tactical execution topics found on the personal legacy plan and learn how to navigate the plan form.

Below are the personal legacy tactical execution areas. Rank them from 1-11 in terms of how much thought you have put into each one, with 1 being the area where you have already invested the most thought and preparation and 11 being the area you have considered least.

_____ **Legal**   _____ **Financial**   _____ **Planned Giving**

_____ **Taxes**   _____ **Insurance**   _____ **Spiritual/Last Remains**

_____ **Advisors**   _____ **Information/Records** _____ **Stewardship**

_____ **Digital Footprint** (What happens to your social media accounts, etc?)

_____ **Communication** (What would you like to communicate to loved ones?)

Now let's examine the table you will see in the plan template.
There is a table for each of the 11 tactical areas with suggestions of items to consider.

Mark the _Yes_ or _No_ column for each item to demonstrate whether or not you have considered that item. In the _Anyone to Influence?_ column, write the names of those with whom you would like to have a conversation about this item and its potential impact on your legacy or on theirs. This column may be empty for many items. As you develop your legacy plan, you can bless others by encouraging them to take similar steps. This may be a spouse, an adult child, an aging parent, a friend, etc.

Have you considered...	YES	NO	ANYONE TO INFLUENCE?	NOTES
Sample Tactical Item				

The tactical side of legacy is not as emotional but is equally important. Taking the time to erect these guardrails is loving your family well.

> A society grows great when old men plant trees whose shade they know they shall never sit in.
>
> – Greek Proverb

Financial Considerations

Begin this lesson by reading the quote in the sidebar and reflecting on this wisdom about legacy.

When the Sorensen family patriarch passed away in the summer of 2012, one aspect of Dale's personal legacy was quickly apparent: he had planned and prepared well for his wife and family. Dale had created his financial plan as a young man and prepared for his passing while he was still in the prime of his life. He intentionally executed on his financial plan, and it provided himself and his wife Ruth with the freedom that comes with having sufficient finances, so they could achieve their life and legacy goals.

Upon his passing, Dale's plan provided his adult children with the peace of knowing that their mother would be well cared for because their father had prepared. He created a legacy that took away the need for his bride of almost 65 years to worry about finances or a place to live. He had invested time in collecting the necessary paperwork and writing down the details of where money was invested and where key pieces of information were stored. Since the details were all in one place, his family was free to focus on the business of remembering and celebrating his life.

In a prior lesson, you took the crucial step of beginning to think about your personal legacy from an ideological perspective of your impact. In this lesson, we turn to the practical side of legacy and examine one of the tactical areas: finances. This will take time and considerable thought to complete thoroughly, but this lesson will get you started on that process.

Which of the following are benefits experienced by the Sorensen family because of Dale's fore-thought and careful planning?

❏ Peace of mind

❏ Adequate finances

❏ Carefree celebration of his life

❏ Freedom to achieve their dreams

Look back at your mission statement and personal legacy statement. Get back into 'dream mode.'

Defining Your Personal Wealth Target (PWT)

A personal wealth target is a goal that defines how much money you would like to have accumulated by the time you leave the workforce.

Some financial planners suggest taking your current annual spending times a multiple of 25-40.

The high multiple is a protective estimate that takes into account factors such as future inflation and the uncertain future of governmental provision for retirees.

What is your personal wealth target (PWT)? How much money do you need to accumulate by the time you leave the workforce in order to live out your post-working life well and leave the legacy you desire?

Assess Today's Financial State

Take a 'snapshot' of your current finances. Make an honest assessment of your financial situation so that you can set accurate goals. While you can do this independently, a financial planner can also help you assess your current financial situation and assist you in setting appropriate goals to reach your envisioned future.

Assets (Something owned that will provide future economic benefit)	
• **Business** (For business owners—this includes the current value of your business as well as things like cash, assets you would monetize on exit such as a building or company vehicles, etc.)	
• **Personal**	
Liabilities (Obligations including money owed or services that must be performed)	
• **Business** (For business owners)	
• **Personal**	
Personal Net Worth (Assets – Liabilities)	

If you do not currently live on a budget, complete a Monthly Cash Flow Plan to track your spending for several months. Do you have a surplus or a deficit?

> With the black and white evidence of your Monthly Cash Flow Plan in front of you, assess your relationship to money. In the past three months my use of money has been…

❑ Wise   ❑ Out of control

❑ Foolish   ❑ Intentional

If you have been foolish with money in the past and feel that your spending is out of control in some areas, don't be upset. It is good that you are identifying those habits now and bringing order to your finances so that you can make your money work for you rather than the other way around. On the other hand, if you have a good relationship with money and can begin to harness the benefits of your money to help you reach your goals, congratulations.

Determining the Gap

What is the gap between your Personal Wealth Target (PWT) and the personal wealth you have currently accumulated?

How big is your personal wealth GAP?

PWT = $ _____

- Personal Net Worth = $ _____

PERSONAL WEALTH GAP = $ _____

There are certain things that are fundamental to human fulfillment. The essence of these needs is captured in the phrase 'to live, to love, to learn, to leave a legacy.' The need to live is our physical need for such things as food, clothing, shelter, economical well-being, health. The need to love is our social need to relate to other people, to belong, to love, and to be loved. The need to learn is our mental need to develop and grow. And the need to leave a legacy is our spiritual need to have a sense of meaning, purpose, personal congruence, and contribution.

– Stephen Covey

What is your timeline to close the GAP?

Year you plan to leave the workforce: _____

                         - Current year: _____

                         TIMELINE GAP = _____ **years**

How much do you need to grow your personal wealth annually to meet your target according to your timeline?

                         PWT GAP = $ _____

                         ÷ TIMELINE GAP = _____ years

ANNUAL PERSONAL WEALTH GROWTH GOAL = $ _____ **per year**

IN SUMMARY
- My Personal Wealth Target (PWT) is $ _____ .

- I have _____ years left to meet my target.

- I need to growth my personal wealth annually by $ _____ .

Are you a business owner who is anticipating selling your company for a handsome payout? Is business value a part of your plan to close the gap in your personal wealth plan? If so, the lesson on the Business Value Target (BVT) in a later chapter will help you calculate an accurate BVT and consider an important fallacy many people hold around the value of their company.

Gathering Financial Information

It is important to gather your financial information about different accounts and investments into one place, such as a three-ring binder, so that loved ones could access the information in the untimely event that you become incapacitated or pass away.

To help with this information gathering, we have created a spreadsheet called the *Personal Legacy Planner* which provides a current snapshot of your finances, places to keep track of financial information, and information about insurance policies. It has a sheet devoted to keeping track of passwords and other important access codes and a sheet to help you think through planning your funeral. A copy of the spreadsheet is posted in the Resource Library. Make sure to share the password to the worksheet with your spouse or someone who will be helping your spouse if you pass away, such as your attorney or executor).

*APPLICATION: **So What? Now What?** You calculated the gap that exists between where you currently are financially and where you would like to be. How will you close that gap? What is your annual plan to grow your personal wealth? Spend some time setting financial goals to walk toward financial freedom so that finances are not what keep you from living toward your legacy.*

Legal Considerations

Begin this lesson by reading the quote in the sidebar and reflecting on this wisdom about legacy.

When a person dies, everything they own is called their estate. A will is an important part of many estate plans. A will is a legally binding document that expresses an individual's wishes for what he or she would like to happen to his/her assets after death.

A will transfers assets through a court-supervised process, called estate administration or probate, which varies from state to state. A will can transfer any asset: cash, personal property (such as family heirlooms or stock certificates), and real estate.

Another role for a will in certain states is to designate specific responsible adults who will serve as custodians for minor children in the event that both parents pass away in a simultaneous tragedy, such as a car accident.

The importance of an up-to-date will cannot be overstated:

- It provides legally binding clarity about your wishes.

- A will can help your family avoid potential conflict and hard feelings.

- It can help provide for the care of your surviving dependents or cover specific needs which may minimize financial hardships.

- If you die without a will, your state law controls the distribution of your assets which may not be as you would choose.

Why is it important to have a legal will? List several benefits.

_____

What are some possible consequences of not having a will?

_____

How do you create a will? Begin by gathering necessary information and thinking through your wishes:

1. *Make a list of your assets, the value of each asset and how the asset is titled (Who are the owners?).* Include your bank accounts, investment accounts, stocks, bonds, life insurance, any real estate, valuable personal property, etc.

2. *Decide the 3 W's: Who, What, and When.*

    a. Whom do you want to inherit?
    b. What would you like them to inherit?

      c. When would you like them to inherit it? (For example, you may want to leave a piece of heirloom jewelry to a daughter on her wedding day. Or you may want to set up a trust for your child to get access to their inheritance on their 21st birthday)

      d. How would you like them to receive it?

3. *Choose a custodian/guardian for your minor children.* It is wise to have an alternate in mind in case the first declines or becomes unable to serve.

4. *Choose an executor.* This person will be charged with carrying out your wishes and handling the paperwork after you die.

5. *Choose a trustee (if needed).* A trustee manages your assets for your beneficiaries after your death.

6. *Contact an attorney or use an online service to create your will which complies with your state law.* Put your will in a safe place and tell your chosen executor as well as your spouse/close friends where it is located.

Other Legal Documents

In addition to a will, there are other legal documents you may wish to consider as part of an effective estate plan:

- *Durable Healthcare Power of Attorney* which allows someone you designate to make healthcare decisions on your behalf if you are incapacitated.

- *Authorization to Release Protected Healthcare Information* allows the doctors, hospitals, and insurance companies to speak with your designee.

- *Living Will (Declaration Regarding Life Support)* explains what medical services, especially life support, you wish to receive if you are incapacitated.

- *Durable General Power of Attorney* authorizes your designee to make general personal business and financial decisions on your behalf, if you are incapacitated.

APPLICATION: Think about your family and friends who have passed on before you. Who did an admirable job in preparing for their passing? What did you admire about his/her preparation?

_____

_____

_____

Create Your Personal Legacy Plan

Begin your study by examining the diagram below.

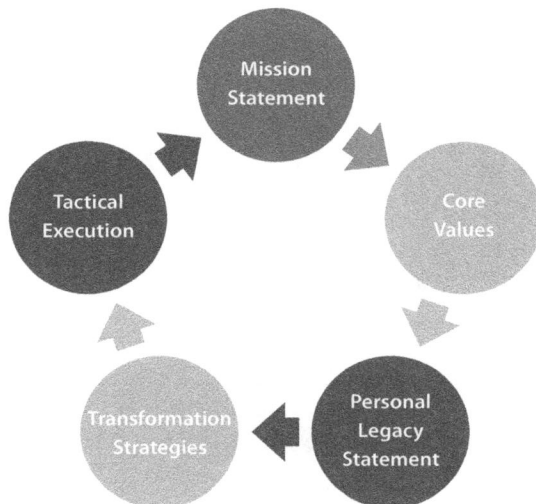

Mission Statement

Core Values

Tactical Execution

Personal Legacy Statement

Transformation Strategies

Hopefully, as you examined the diagram, you will notice that all of your hard work this week has paid off! Your legacy plan is almost complete. Today we will simply put the pieces together.

This has been a challenging week. Which piece was hardest?

- ❏ Mission
- ❏ Transformation Strategies
- ❏ Personal Legacy Statement
- ❏ Financial Considerations (Determining your PWT)
- ❏ Will and Other Legal Documents

Fill out the Personal Legacy Plan which you see on the next page. To fill it out electronically, you can download the plan templates for all Four Plans in the Resource Library. The first page deals with your impact. You can look back at the lessons in this chapter to find the information you need to compile as you fill out this page of the template. The subsequent pages focus on the tactical side of your personal legacy.

APPLICATION: Write down one good outcome that will come from the challenging work you have put in creating your legacy plan.

_____

_____

_____

Personal Legacy Plan

HUNDREDFOLD Harvest

Name

Company

Year

PERSONAL MISSION	PERSONAL VALUES

DOMAINS
If these suggested domains do not fit you, feel free to change them to align with your situation.

PERSONAL LEGACY STATEMENT
What impact do you want your life to have in each domain? Write 2-3 sentences per domain.

TRANSFORMATION STRATEGIES
How will you ignite transformation in this domain? Note a high-level strategy for each domain.

DOMAINS	PERSONAL LEGACY STATEMENT	TRANSFORMATION STRATEGIES
Personal		
Family		
Career		
Spiritual		
Community		

Financial Targets	*Personal Wealth Target*	$	*Years to Target*
	Current Net Worth	$	

TACTICAL EXECUTION

This document highlights areas or gaps where you may need to execute your legacy plan and for accountability in your peer group. Click the arrow next to each category to see suggested action items. The Influence column is to remind you to encourage others do their own legacy planning (parents, in-laws, adult children, employees, etc.).

LEGAL

Update where you are on each of these legal strategies.	*Have you considered…*	YES	NO	ANYONE TO INFLUENCE?	NOTES
	Wills, Trusts, POD (will substitutes)				
	Caretakers for minor children				
	Durable Power of Attorney				
	Advanced Directive (living will)				
	Healthcare Power of Attorney				
	Organ Donation				

FINANCIAL

Update where you are on each of these financial considerations.	*Have you considered…*	YES	NO	ANYONE TO INFLUENCE?	NOTES
	401K/IRA				
	SEP/SERP				
	529 Plan				
	Stocks, Bonds, Mutual Funds				
	Real Estate				

PLANNED GIVING

Update where you are on planning monetary giving.

Have you considered...	YES	NO	ANYONE TO INFLUENCE?	NOTES
Charitable Contributions				

TAXES

Update where you are on each of these tax considerations.

Have you considered...	YES	NO	ANYONE TO INFLUENCE?	NOTES
Estate/Inheritance Tax Planning				
Income Tax Planning				

INSURANCE

Update where you are on each of these insurance considerations.

Have you considered...	YES	NO	ANYONE TO INFLUENCE?	NOTES
Risk Management: *Personal Liability Umbrella*				
Life Insurance				
Disability Insurance				
Health Insurance				
Long Term Care Insurance				

STEWARDSHIP

Update where you are on each of these considerations about stewarding what you have well.

Think about how you can utilize your time and talents in each domain, especially the Community domain.

Have you considered…	YES	NO	ANYONE TO INFLUENCE?	NOTES
Time How do you want to invest your time to achieve your desired legacy?				
Talent What are your unique talents? How will you cultivate and use those talents to benefit others?				
Treasure What do you plan to do with your assets? Sketch out a high level plan here. You will deal with the legal implications of this strategy under Tactical Execution in the next phase.				

SPIRITUAL/LAST REMAINS

Update where you are on each of these considerations regarding final arrangements.

Have you considered…	YES	NO	ANYONE TO INFLUENCE?	NOTES
Pre-paid funeral arrangements or other disposition of last remains				
Pre-planned service				
TOOL: Funeral Preferences tab in the Legacy Planner Spreadsheet				
Eternity – your personal relationship with God or what is sacred to you				

DIGITAL FOOTPRINT

Update where you are on managing and making plans to eradicate your digital footprint.

Have you considered...	YES	NO	ANYONE TO INFLUENCE?	NOTES
Social media/blogs/pictures/data				

COMMUNICATION

Update where you are on each of these communication considerations.

Have you considered...	YES	NO	ANYONE TO INFLUENCE?	NOTES
Your Loved Ones				
What do I need to communicate to those I love? (values I want to pass on, etc)				
How will I communicate it? (video, letters to family members, etc)				
Stakeholders				
Who is vested in your success and lasting impact? Who needs to know about this legacy plan?				
Executor				
Do you have your info stored in one location where your executor can find it?				

ADVISORS

Update where you are on each of these relationships with experts in their field who can help you with your legacy.

Have you considered...	YES	NO	ANYONE TO INFLUENCE?	NOTES
Bank/Broker/Financial Advisor				
Attorney				
CPA				
Insurance Agent				
Spiritual Advisor (Pastor/Priest/Discipler/Mentor)				

INFORMATION/RECORDS

Update your passwords, account info, etc. on a regular basis so that all of the information is in one place.

Have you updated your...	YES	NO	ANYONE TO INFLUENCE?	NOTES
Personal Legacy Planner (Spreadsheet)				

Chapter 2: Notes

Life Plan

Life is a gift. None of us chose to be born; even the most determined and strong-willed among us must admit that we had nothing to do with our birth. We would also commonly acknowledge that we have little to do with continuing to draw breath each day.

There are many things that are true about life:

- We receive only one.
- We each get the same 168 hours a week.
- Life is finite.

In his book, *The Principle of the Path*, pastor and author Andy Stanley reminds us, "Direction—not intentions, hopes, dreams, prayers, beliefs, intellect, or education—determines destination."

The decisions that we make in our lives, from the big decisions to the small, put us on a path that will take us to a destination.

In the prior chapter on personal legacy, we spent time dreaming and determining what our desired destination will be. In this chapter, you will create your life plan to flesh out the path you will walk toward your legacy in the next year.

CHAPTER 3 LESSONS

Anchoring Your Life

What's Important Now?

Life-Work Tension

Prepare to Be Accountable

Create Your Life Plan

Anchoring Your Life

Begin this lesson by reading the quote in the sidebar and reflecting on this wisdom about life planning.

To create the legacy plan we began with the end in mind. We wrote our legacy statement which paints a vision 20 years down the road of a life well lived. It describes what we want the impact of our life to be.

Our focus now shifts to the life plan. The Life Plan is where you plan the intentional next steps you will take toward your desired legacy. In this chapter, we will take the legacy plan's high-level vision and create goals.

Take a moment to look back at your legacy plan.

Write your legacy statement below to remind you of your desired ultimate reality.

_____

_____

Write your personal mission statement here.

_____

_____

Write your personal core values below.

1. _____   2. _____   3. _____

4. _____   5. _____

As we set off on this journey of mapping our life for the next year, it is important that we keep the compass of our core values firmly in hand, being mindful of them and checking every goal and action plan for alignment.

We want to make sure we are looking through the lens of our mission, legacy statement, and core values as we endeavor to plan our lives. They are the anchor that will keep us from drifting toward things that seem exciting or urgent in the moment but utimately distract us from our desired legacy.

APPLICATION: Reflect on the idea of the mission, legacy statement, and values being an anchor. How do you agree/disagree with this analogy?

What's Important Now?

Begin this lesson by reading the quote in the sidebar and reflecting on this wisdom about life planning.

Determining Your Priorities

As mentioned in the introductory paragraph for this week, we each get 168 hours in a week. Time (like death and taxes) is an equalizer in life. Rich or poor, educated or illiterate, whether you are living for yourself or pouring out your life on behalf of others, you get 168 hours.

We are not going to delve into this exercise right now, but a helpful first step is to record how you spend your time for a week or even a month. It reveals patterns and areas of waste as well as areas where you want to devote more time. If you have never tracked how you are spending your time, it is a valuable and simple effort. It is always eye-opening.

In this lesson, we are going to focus on prioritizing. There are many different demands on your time, so it is vital that you (using your core values as a guide) prioritize the areas where you want to devote time. Then you can live intentionally. There will always be more things to do than time to do them which results in tension. The life plan provides a mechanism to keep you focused on the things that matter.

Look back at your legacy plan. Copy the transformation strategies on the lines below, one strategy per line.

Note the domain and then the strategy. There are five domains, so you should have at least five strategies. If you have multiple strategies for a domain, give each strategy its own line. Draw additional boxes and lines as needed.

I'll do one as an example for you. |2| *Personal: Practice hobbies* _____

Ask yourself the question, "What's Important NOW?" Rank the transformation strategies in order of their priority for you currently.

Put a 1 in the box next to the strategy of highest importance, and an 8 next to the strategy of least importance currently.

There are no right or wrong answers! All of the strategies remain options to pursue throughout the whole year. You are just prioritizing which to pursue first.

	_____
	_____
	_____

> *If we would only give the same amount of reflection to what we want out of life as we give to the question of what to do with two weeks' vacation, we would be startled at our false standards and the aimless procession of our busy days.*
>
> – Dorothy Canfield Fisher

☐ _____

☐ _____

☐ _____

☐ _____

☐ _____

Setting Goals in the Life Domains and Planning for Action

You have determined your areas of priority. The next step is to write each of the top three to four transformation strategies in the form of a SMART goal. Remember that SMART goals are Specific, Measurable, Achievable, Relevant, and Time-Bound.

Here is an example goal based on the transformation strategy given above:

Domain	SMART Goal	Action Plan
Personal	Practice woodworking by taking an eight-week online class starting in March and creating a project quarterly using what I learned in the class.	• Select class • Sign up & attend • List potential projects • Make projects

Your turn. Take three of your transformation strategies listed above and write them here as goals. You may have multiple goals for one domain and no goals for another. That is okay. Remember at any one time your life plan goals reflect what is currently important. That may emphasize one domain over another. Over time, however, you will want to be sure you are moving forward in every domain.

Domain	SMART Goal	Action Plan

Once you have written the goals, add an action plan with three to four steps you need to take to attain each goal.

Breaking each goal down into bite-sized steps will help you accomplish them. It will make what seems daunting feel more achievable, building your confidence and motivation to work toward that goal.

Planning to Execute

Intentions do not determine your destination. Planning is only part of the equation; we must frequently review and execute on plans to ensure the direction they are leading will bring us to our desired destination.

Thomas Edison said, "Vision without execution is hallucination." Perhaps you have been hallucinating in these different areas you noted above where you would like to see transformation in your life. You may feel skeptical about following through on your life plan because the path of your personal experience is littered with abandoned goals and objectives. You may feel fear at the thought of failing again. Or you may feel excitement and anticipation about your goals.

Reflect for a moment on what you are feeling and write a sentence or two explaining why you are experiencing that particular emotion as you think about executing on your goals.

_____

_____

Most people struggle, whether they acknowledge it or not, to execute consistently and well in every area of life. Goals we attempt usually fall in one of two categories:

- Those we have full control over (such as purchasing a new set of furniture)
- Those we have partial control over (gathering your family together for a weekly family night)

Both goals require something of you in terms of time, money, or effort, but those goals that require behavioral change and the involvement of other people are the most daunting. However, they may also bring the greatest reward.

People who execute effectively have five things in common:

1. A clear understanding of their goal and how to go about reaching it
2. A strong commitment to their goal and intrinsic motivation to work toward achieving it
3. A consistent accountability relationship to keep them focused
4. A willingness to take personal responsibility for their actions
5. A regular practice of measuring their progress toward their goals

APPLICATION: Read the statements above. Circle the numbers of the two statements you feel you already do well. Underline the statement you would like to describe you in the future.

> Each hour we are blessed to live is not a disconnected 60 minutes. It is a small slice of our legacy – and as a result needs to tie into our WHY and connect with the overall vision of where we are going.
> – Arlin Sorensen

Life-Work Tension

There is a continual battle to balance life and work, but this idealistic aim is not realistic. We will never achieve perfect balance.

There will be seasons when life at home requires more attention and energy, be it during a move or after the birth of a new baby, etc. Likewise, there will be times when work will require more attention and energy.

Instead of talking about life-work balance, we prefer to talk about life-work tension. Our hope is to raise awareness that it exists for each of us. When we are mindful of this tension, we can begin to manage it and keep our focus on our priorities. We are also more likely to offer ourselves and others grace. This involves recognizing life is seasonal, and the tension will occasionally pull more to one side than the other.

Without a plan, we find ourselves defaulting to the urgent rather than executing on the important.

We allow the tyranny of the urgent to rule our days, resulting in the exact outcome described by Dorothy Canfield Fisher in her quote in the prior lesson: we drift. Our busy days become "an aimless procession," passing us by without taking us in a purposeful direction.

Never confuse having a career with having a life. This is a vital precept to keep in mind as you prioritize and commit to live out your life in accordance with your core values. Read the bold line above and then the quote in the margin… aloud (seriously, reading aloud helps you to listen). Then synthesize the two messages in your own words below.

_____

_____

APPLICATION: How are you doing with your life-work tension? Put an X in the appropriate spot on the continuum below.

WORK ⟵——————————————————————————⟶ **LIFE**

Explain your answer.

_____

_____

_____

_____

Prepare to Be Accountable

Begin this lesson by reading the quote in the sidebar and reflecting on this wisdom about consistent execution.

Accountability involves being responsible for your choices and actions.

Accountability partners and peer groups play a significant role. We all need a community at times to keep us encouraged and focused. However, at the end of the day, you are the one who will achieve your goals.

On the Life Plan form, there is a column titled Status and one titled Target Date. These equip your accountability partners to help you succeed.

In the status column, you 'stoplight' your pacing and progress.

- **Green** indicates you are on pace to achieve your goal by the target date.

- **Yellow** indicates you are slightly off pace; there is a possibility you may not achieve your goal by the target date.

- **Red** indicates either you are stalled due to a roadblock or you will not achieve your goal by the target date.

The target date column should be filled in with the date by which you commit to complete the goal.

To end this lesson on accountability, we are going to outline questions we can ask ourselves and equip our accountability partners to verify whether we are on track to achieve our goal.

APPLICATION: Look back at your three to four SMART goals you created in the previous lesson. Write a question for each goal you can answer to verify whether you have achieved that goal. How will you know you have succeeded?

Using the example goal from the prior lesson, accountability questions could be as follows: Did I take the online woodworking class? Did I create a woodworking project each quarter?

_____

_____

_____

_____

_____

> *Every day do something that will inch you closer to a better tomorrow.*
>
> *– Doug Firebaugh*

Create Your Life Plan

If you don't design your own life plan, chances are you'll fall into someone else's plan. And guess what they have planned for you? Not much.

– Jim Rohn

Begin this lesson by reading the quote in the sidebar and reflecting on this wisdom about planning.

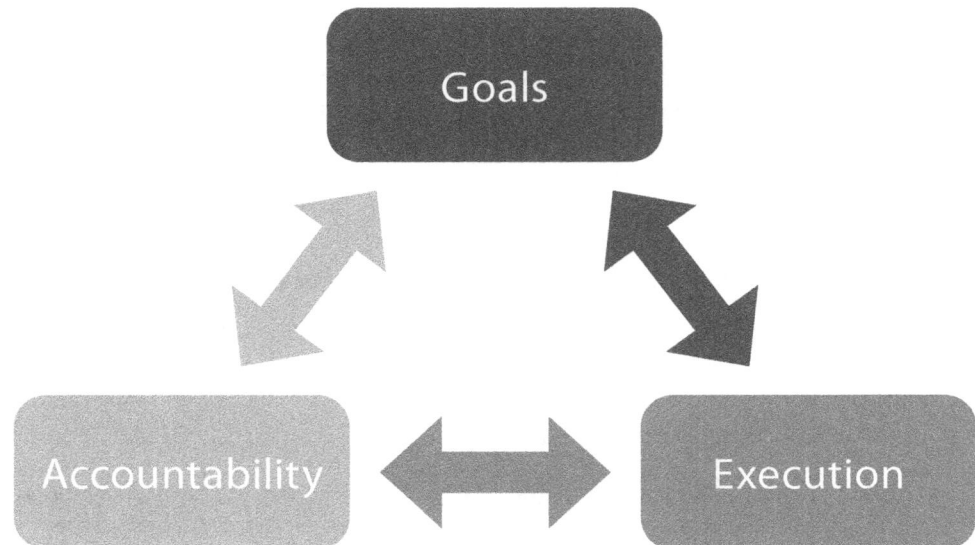

Goals

Accountability

Execution

Hopefully, as you examined the diagram, you will notice that your work has paid off! Your life plan is almost complete. In this lesson, we will simply put the pieces together as you compile the appropriate items from your work in this chapter into one plan. This is a format that is easy to monitor and share.

A life plan enables us to live proactively rather than just letting life happen to us and waking up one day to find out that we are in a place we have no desire to be.

Planning allows us to make sure that we focus on doing the things we can control and not worrying about things outside of our control.

You may have heard it said that life is what happens while we are busy making plans. Having a plan is what frees us up to live present and rejoice in the spontaneous moments that make up our lives.

The legacy plan identifies our desired direction. The life plan puts in place the tangible steps we begin taking to get there.

Congratulations on taking the time to write a life plan. Share it with those you love. Review it regularly and ensure that you are walking toward your goals. But most importantly, LIVE. Life is a gift.

Life Plan

Name

Company

Year

PERSONAL MISSION	PERSONAL LEGACY STATEMENT	PERSONAL VALUES

DOMAIN	SMART GOAL	ACTION PLAN	STATUS	TARGET DATE

PWT	Current Net Worth	Net Worth at Year End	Years to Target

Chapter 3: Notes

_____

_____

_____

_____

_____

_____

_____

_____

_____

_____

_____

_____

_____

_____

_____

_____

_____

_____

_____

_____

_____

_____

_____

_____

CHAPTER 4

Business Legacy Plan

Leaving a business legacy is about what lives beyond your tenure with your company, not only in terms of the financial details of what you leave behind but more importantly in terms of the lives you have impacted through your leadership.

The previous chapter explored the topic of personal legacy and led you to create a personal legacy plan. You authored a personal legacy statement which answers the questions, "How will my life impact others? The world?"

In this chapter, we will again examine the question of legacy, only this time from a business perspective.

This is a plan that should be collaboratively developed if you have business partners.

Each of you will have a different answer for how leading the company will affect you personally. However, for the other four domains, you will work together to write a business legacy statement that answers the question, "How will our company impact others? Our community?"

CHAPTER 4 LESSONS

Craft a Company Mission Statement

Craft a Company Vision Statement

Write a Business Legacy Statement

Transformation Strategies

Guardrails for Business Legacy

Disaster Recovery

Planning for Transition or Exit

Business Value

Create Your Business Legacy Plan

Craft a Company Mission Statement

There will always be more good ideas than there is capacity to execute.

– Sean Covey

Begin this lesson by reading the quote in the sidebar and reflecting on this wisdom about legacy.

A mission statement bears in mind your corporate values and answers the question, "Why does this company exist?" It is a statement of purpose, providing the parameters that help you focus your efforts for maximum success.

Think of the mission statement as an expression of an organization's leadership. It conveys their desires and intent for the organization. It focuses and directs the organization itself, communicating both to the employees who work for the company and to customers and partners who work with the company.

Read these examples of mission statements.

3M	To solve unsolved problems innovatively.
Arby's	To provide an exceptional dining experience that satisfies our guests' grown-up tastes by being a 'Cut-Above' in everything we do.
Ben & Jerry's Ice Cream	To make, distribute, and sell the finest quality all-natural ice cream and euphoric concoctions with a continued commitment to incorporating wholesome, natural ingredients and promoting business practices that respect the Earth and the environment.
eBay	Provide a global trading platform where practically anyone can trade practically anything.
Harley-Davidson, Inc	We fulfill dreams through the experience of motorcycling, by providing to motorcyclists and to the general public an expanding line of motorcycles and branded products and services in selected market segments.
Lowe's	Helping customers improve the places they call home.
Mary Kay Cosmetics	To give unlimited opportunity to women.
Ritz Carlton Hotels	We are Ladies and Gentlemen serving Ladies and Gentlemen.
Starbucks	To inspire and nurture the human spirit—one person, one cup, and one neighborhood at a time.
Warby Parker	To offer designer eyewear at a revolutionary price, while leading the way for socially-conscious businesses.
Wal-Mart	To save people money so they can live better.
Zappos	To provide the best customer service possible.

Consider the following questions and make some general notes next to each mission statement:

- Which mission statements make you think, "Wow! That fits with what I know of that company"?

- Which statements help you to understand a company more fully and why they make certain decisions?

- How is the length—too long, too short, just right?

- What business is this company in?

- If you were an employee, would you find this mission compelling?

- Who is their target customer?

What criteria do you want to keep in mind as you develop your mission statement? (Some criteria may include: short, memorable, inspiring, market-focused, unique)

_____

_____

> *Work is about the search, too, for daily meaning as well as daily bread, for recognition, as well as for cash, for astonishment rather than torpor, in short, for a sort of life rather than a Monday through Friday sort of dying.*
>
> *– Studs Terkel*

Craft a Company Mission Statement

A mission statement is a timeless one-sentence statement that is clear and easily remembered, so no further explanation is needed. A corporate mission statement often consists of four parts:

- Why does our company exist?
- Whom do we want to serve?

- What value will we provide?
- What is the result?

Here is an example of a corporate mission statement:
We will inspire thriving communities by connecting people to the technology that makes business easy.

Step 1: Get employee input.

You can send an email out to your team and ask them to tell you stories, "What do we do when we are doing our best work? Whom do we serve? How do we serve them? What do we offer? Why do we exist?"

Their wording can be helpful input in the brainstorming process. Take adjectives and nouns from the team's suggestions and group them to determine who you serve, what you do, and why.

Write their answers in this table. Then, answer each question in a sentence.

• According to a
2017 Gallup study,
engaged employees
have 41% lower
absenteeism than
non-engaged
and are 17% more
productive.[1]

• The #1 way
to minimize
disengagement?
Focus on your
shared mission.

Why does our company exist?	Whom do we serve?	How do we serve them?	What do we offer?
Top answers: • • •	Top answers: • • •	Top answers: • • •	Top answers: • • •
Sentence:	Sentence:	Sentence:	Sentence:

Now bring those thoughts together into a concise mission statement. You can do this in different ways. One effective way is to have everyone around the table draft one or two mission statements independently using the stories employees have told and the information on purpose, target customer persona, etc. that you have already gathered. Then come back together and discuss. Often it is a combination of one or two different ideas that make a strong mission statement.

Another idea is to list single adjectives or nouns that you believe could be included in the mission statement on sticky notes and post them on a white board. Group words that are similar and ask what they have in common. Then move the sticky notes around. Use a marker and blank sticky notes, filling in the rest of the words to make it a complete statement. Try using the words in several diverse ways.

DRAFT - COMPANY MISSION STATEMENT

_____

_____

Step 2: Get feedback.

There can be a rosy haze over a mission statement when it is first written because so much work has gone into crafting it. It is wise to step back from it for a period of time and solicit honest feedback.

- Ask employees if they understand the mission statement and if it motivates them.

- Ask customers if they would want to do business with a company that is working to accomplish the mission you describe.

- Ask vendor partners if they understand how their product or service enables you accomplishing your mission.

Take the feedback you gathered from employees, customers, and vendor partners and revise your mission statement.

Step 3: Wait a bit longer.

Perhaps put aside your revised mission statement for another few weeks and don't look at it. Then come back and read it with fresh eyes.

- Does it express the reason the company exists?

- Is it concise? Does it pass the Twitter test (168 characters or less)?

- Is it compelling? Does it motivate people to come to work each day?

- Is it catchy? Will it stick with people long after having read it?

Does it answer the four questions?

- Why does our company exist?

- Whom do we want to serve?

- What value will we provide?

- What is the result?

As you assess your mission statement, if your answer to any of these questions is negative, take the time to go back and continue revising the statement until it is something you have confidence in sharing publicly.

In some cases there may be an internal and an external version of the mission statement—one for the team to connect with and a second for customers and vendor partners. It depends on the outcome of your work. Recognize that it is possible to have two versions, both of which have the same meaning, but stated through two different viewpoints.

Step 4: Finalize your mission statement and share it publicly.

Once you have your final mission statement, display it in your office, on your website, etc. Let people know that you are a mission-driven company that exists for a specific purpose.

OUR COMPANY MISSION STATEMENT

_____

_____

Don't forget to take a moment and celebrate as a team! You now have a mission statement.

Point out to employees how they individually make a difference, how their actions affect others and help the company succeed. This can result in behavior that transcends self.

Craft a Company Vision Statement

A vision statement paints a picture of the business's envisioned future three to five years down the road. It answers the question, "Where are you headed?"

Step 1: Get team input.

Start out by having each person on the strategic planning team write down their own vision. Consider your revenue size, what your culture people development will look like, whom you will be serving, how you will serve them, and your desired outcome.

As I look through the telescope, this is the company I see...

Three years down the road

Five years down the road

Give several people a chance to share their vision for different points in the future. Then begin to explore some of the questions posed in the margin. Use the answers to the questions to fill in the following chart.

Timeframe	Geographical Scope (New markets)	Products and Services (New offerings)	Type of Business (New model)	Other Aspirations (Short-term dreams)
Three year				
Five year				

DRAFT - COMPANY VISION STATEMENT

Step 2: Get feedback.

As with a mission statement, there can be a rosy haze over a vision statement when it is first written. It is wise to step back from it for a period and solicit honest feedback.

- Ask employees if they understand the vision statement and if it excites them to be part of building that future.

- Take the feedback you gathered from employees and revise your vision.

Step 3: Wait a bit.

Perhaps put aside your revised vision statement for a few weeks and don't look at it. Then come back and read it with fresh eyes.

- Does it paint a clear picture of the next three to five years? Can people summarize the main points?

- Is it compelling? Do people want to be part of the journey? Is your vision big enough that it is beyond you (and requires the entire team to pull together to accomplish it)?

- Is it consistently modeled and communicated by leaders? Is it shared clearly with the team?

If your answer to any of these questions is negative, continue revising the statement until it is something you have confidence in sharing to answer the question "Where are you going in three to five years?"

Step 4: Finalize your vision statement and share it.

Once you have your final vision statement, share it with your team. Consider whether it is appropriate to share your vision externally with others such as your customers, vendor partners, professional partners perhaps including a banker or attorney or accountant.

OUR COMPANY VISION STATEMENT

APPLICATION: On a scale of 1 to 10 (1 being non-alignment, 10 being perfectly aligned), rate how well your corporate mission statement aligns with your core values. Using the same scale, rate how well your corporate vision statement aligns with these values.

Mission Statement: 1   2   3   4   5   6   7   8   9   10

Vision Statement: 1   2   3   4   5   6   7   8   9   10

> There is a big difference between being an organization with a vision statement and becoming a true visionary organization. The difference lies in creating alignment – alignment to preserve an organization's core values, to reinforce its purpose, and to stimulate continued progress towards its aspirations. When you have superb alignments, a visitor could drop into your organization from another planet and infer the vision without having to read it on paper.
>
> – Jim Collins

Write a Business Legacy Statement

> *You have to know one big thing and stick with it. The leaders who had one very big idea and one very big commitment that permitted them to create something, those are the ones who leave a legacy.*
>
> – Irving Kristol

Begin this lesson by reading the quote in the sidebar and reflecting on this wisdom about legacy.

Just as both the impact of your life on others and the tactical stewardship of your resources are vital parts of a personal legacy, leaving a strong business legacy is also twofold.

- First, a business legacy entails thinking through how the mission and vision of the business will continue even after you are gone.

  The Business Legacy Plan answers the question, "What impact do I want my leadership and the company to have had when I am no longer leading it?"

- Second, leaving a strong business legacy involves thinking through the stewardship and management of company resources, both in the present and to prepare for the future.

In this lesson we will examine the first reason.

Take a moment to consider the task ahead of you as you craft a business legacy plan. What thoughts are racing through your mind?

❏ It's about time we did this.   ❏ I'm overwhelmed.

❏ We're too small for a plan.   ❏ Let's dig in. I'm ready to work.

Whatever you are feeling, we will take this monumental task step-by-step.

It will take months, if not years, to thoroughly complete your business legacy plan. We are not under the illusion that you will complete the entire plan right now.

Hopefully, by the end of these lessons, you will have sufficient resources and information to give you a strong start on your plan.

Part 1: Understanding the Business Domains

Just as we talk about five life domains, we also talk about five business domains that are applicable to most companies. These are suggested domains. If one does not apply, please feel free to substitute a different domain in its place.

Personal: Think of the Personal domain in terms of your own leadership of the company. What kind of leader do you want to be?

Business Partners: The business partners domain includes co-owners of the company or other stakeholders.

Employees: This domain includes those who work for the company.

Customers/Vendors: This domain pertains to those who purchase products or services from your company (customers) and those whose products and services you sell or license (vendors).

Community: This domain includes your company's impact on the local community, business organizations to which you belong (such as the chamber of commerce), and other philanthropic efforts.

APPLICATION: Reflect on each of the five business domains. Using the definitions given above, fill in the chart showing who and what would fall into each of your business domains.

Business Domain	Defining My Business Domains
Personal	
Business Partner(s)	
Employees	
Customers/Vendors	
Community	

Part 2: Writing a Business Legacy Statement

Write your company mission statement below.

_____

_____

With your mission statement fresh in your mind, let's begin to draft your business legacy statement.

Dream a bit and imagine the company a year before your exit.

Give yourself the grace to picture the company with both you and your colleagues having lived your corporate mission statement out faithfully every single day spanning that time between now and your exit from leadership.

Questions to keep in mind as you craft your business legacy statement:

- *Who is my target audience?*
    - *Employees*
    - *A future generation of employees*
    - *Your partners, future business owner*

- *How do I want the mission, vision, and values of the organization I led to live on after my tenure with the company ends?*

- *What relational impact do I want our company to have?*

- *What impact do I want my leadership to have?*

In the table below, record one to two sentences for each domain describing what that domain has become. Use present tense, writing from the perspective of what will be true one year before you exit. Allow the question under the domain name to serve as a prompt.

Business Domain	Describe Each Business Domain a Year Before You Exit *If you and your team live your corporate mission out in this domain faithfully… what would happen?*
Personal *Who are you as a leader? (Describe your style, how you show up as a leader, your actions as you have led the company according to its mission. If there are multiple partners, each of you will have a different statement for the personal domain.)*	
Business Partner(s) *Who are you as partners because you lived out this mission together?*	
Employees *What is true of your employees because they worked at this company?*	
Customers/Vendors *Describe your relationship with your customers and vendors as a result of doing business together.*	
Community *What has happened in your communities because your company and team were a part of them?*	

Read back over your draft as if it were written as one paragraph and verify that it is written in the present tense.

Sometimes this exercise is easier with an example. The following example was crafted after imagining a leader and his team had lived out this company mission consistently day-in and day-out until his exit: *We will inspire thriving communities by connecting people to the technology that makes business easy.*

Here is an example of a business legacy statement:

I am a leader who builds other leaders. I care deeply about my team and have learned when to remain silent and when to coach. I have helped each of my direct reports to grow beyond my own level of success as they built their own teams.

Our partners enable our personal legacies because we create a business that is valuable and sustainable. We will be able to sell it for what we need to live comfortably. Our families understand the value of work but see that work is there to support the family, not the family there to support the work.

Our employees give thought to their own lives and legacies. Each one feels invested in by the leadership of our company as we develop them and encourage them to create and live their own legacy plans.

Our customers see in us someone who cares for their success as much as ours.

Our vendor partners trust us as a 'Go-To Partner' who does what we say. We mutually enable one another to be successful. They have a seat at our planning table, and we have a seat on their advisory council as well.

There is a scholarship fund in our community named after our company for those interested in IT. We also volunteer for career fairs at the local high school and encourage our employees to do monthly mentoring of high school students who show interest in business or the IT profession.

Read your business legacy statement one more time through the lens of your business mission statement, company vision, and company core values.

- **Does it align with your mission, vision, and values?**

- **Does it excite and motivate?**

Make any revisions you would like and write your complete business legacy statement below.

_____

_____

APPLICATION: Share the business legacy statement with your partners or leadership team. What feedback do they offer?

_____

_____

Transformation Strategies

Hope is not a strategy.

– Rudy Giuliani

Begin your study by reading and reflecting on the planning wisdom in the margin.

Remember that transformation strategies are the stepping stones between your mission and legacy. They answer the question "How?"

How will this desired impact happen? How will our actions as leaders of the company ignite success in this domain?

Let's review. Transformation strategies are not:

- **Goals.** They are high-level strategies.

- **Lengthy.** They are brief phrases.

- **Set in stone.** These are ideas and suggestions for strategies. You will change these strategies over time to fit your circumstances.

- **Comprehensive.** This initial list may not include all the ways you could or desire to ignite success in a particular domain. You will add to it over time.

Look back at our example business legacy statement and practice coming up with some transformation strategies. I've done the business partner(s) domain for you.

Domain	Business Legacy Statement	Transformation Strategies
Business Partner(s)	*Our partners enable our personal legacies because we create a business that is valuable and sustainable. We will be able to sell it for what we need to live comfortably. Our families understand the value of work but see that work is there to support the family, not the family there to support the work.*	• Plan vacations not around work • Be home at agreed upon time • 'Be present' box: put cell phone away during dinner and family time • Business Value Creation Strategy • Exit Plan

Your Turn. Given a section from our example business legacy statement, fill in the transformation strategies for the Employee Domain.

Domain	Business Legacy Statement	Transformation Strategies
Employees	*Our employees give thought to their own lives and legacies. Each one feels invested in by the leadership of our company as we develop them and encourage them to create and live out their own legacy plans.*	

Now look back at your own business legacy statement and note transformation strategies for each domain. You can copy your business legacy statement below or just flip back and forth to the page where you wrote your statement.

Domain	Business Legacy Statement	Transformation Strategies
Personal		
Business Partner(s)		
Employees		
Customers/ Vendors		
Community		

APPLICATION: As you look over your transformation strategies, which are you most excited to dive into first? Which do you think will make the biggest impact initially?

_____

_____

Guardrails for Business Legacy

Refer to the lesson on establishing guardrails in the personal legacy chapter of this book. Review and summarize the purpose of guardrails.

_____

In terms of business legacy, guardrails are tactical areas that need to be considered to protect the company both in terms of being able to continue day-to-day operations in the face of unforeseen circumstances and in order for the leaders to transition well. It is proactive thinking that sets the company up for success and provides peace of mind for the employees.

There are many tactical areas that one could consider when planning for legacy. In this lesson, we will introduce the nine tactical execution topics found on the Business Legacy Plan and learn how to navigate the plan form.

Below are the business legacy tactical execution areas. Rank them from 1 to 9 in terms of how much thought you have put into each one: 1 being the area where you have already invested the most thought and preparation, 9 being the area you have considered least.

_____ **Legal**   _____ **Taxes**   _____ **Planned Giving**

_____ **Contingency**   _____ **Insurance**   _____ **Exit/Succession Planning**

_____ **Advisors**   _____ **Communication**   _____ **Digital Footprint**

Now let's examine the table you will see in the plan template. There is a table for each of the nine tactical areas with suggestions of items to consider.

Mark the *Yes* or *No* column for each item to demonstrate whether or not you have considered that item. In the *Anyone to Influence?* column, write the names of those with whom you would like to have a conversation about this item and its potential impact on the company's legacy. This may be a business partner, an employee who is charged with oversight of a key area, a family member who needs to consider this, a customer or vendor who needs to take action, etc.

Have you considered...	YES	NO	ANYONE TO INFLUENCE?	NOTES
Sample Tactical Item				

These tactical areas are important to consider so that you do not fail to prepare and thus prepare to fail.

It will take a considerable amount of time to ponder and act upon each area. By dedicating this time, you are putting in place protections that will serve the company well long into the future.

Business Continuity

Begin this lesson by reading the quote in the sidebar and reflecting on this wisdom about the importance of precautionary planning.

You need a plan. Now is the time to decide how to continue in the event something interrupts business. Regardless of your company size or location, you have customers, employees, and stakeholders who are relying on your business to continue operations during and following a disaster. Once disaster strikes, it is too late to plan.

Estimate how long you think it will take you to develop a business continuity plan.

_____

Creating a business continuity and disaster recovery plan does not have to be challenging or time intensive. Some have created it in a day or less. Most of the plan revolves around things you already know and do. It is simply a matter of recording the information and collecting it in a usable format so that it can be stored in a central location.

> *"A good plan executed right now is better than a perfect plan next week."*
>
> -George Patton

On a scale of 1 to 10 (1 being not at all prepared, 10 being well-prepared), rate your own preparation of your company for one of the following: a sudden disaster, brief interruptions to business, or for key personnel to suddenly leave the company.

If something unforeseen were to happen today, how well have you prepared the business?

My Preparation:　　　1　2　3　4　5　6　7　8　9　10

This lesson is designed to prepare you and your business to continue operating in the face of a circumstance that threatens to interrupt business. The data around small business recovery from a disaster is staggering. Over 75% don't have a plan. Somewhere between 40-70% of small businesses fail within two years after a disaster. This is a serious need for all businesses to address.

Philosophy of Business Continuity/Disaster Recovery Planning

1. Focus on the most critical things—people, facilities, operations.

2. Prevent business interruptions whenever possible.

3. Have a plan to address people, facilities, and operations when interruptions occur.

4. Utilize everyday tools whenever possible.

Think through the following events which pose possible interruptions to your ability to carry on daily functions of your business.

Everyone has a moment of panic. The trick is to move past that and begin to figure out where you are and what you should do now. And the best way to do that is to have lived this moment before—in drills and in your imagination. It's not knowing what to do [in case of a disaster] that will save you. It's knowing that you know what to do.

– Ben Sherwood

con·ti·nu·i·ty

/ noun /

1 The process to continue critical business operations during and immediately after a disaster.

Synonyms: constancy, stability, continuum

Think of them as events with short duration. Each of these events has the potential to become a disaster when the duration is lengthened.

Interruption to Business (Short Duration)	Have a plan	No plan yet	Preparing
Loss of Power			
Loss of Internet			
Loss of Phone			
Loss of Cellular Network			
Loss of Critical Server			
Loss of Critical Application			
Loss of Email			
Utility Shut-Off			
Road Construction			
Loss of Key Client			

Business Continuity and Disaster Recovery planning are important for every business, especially for the SMB space where businesses are less likely to have formal plans. This is a value-add you can provide your clients as well once you create your own BC/DR plan and document the planning process yourself.

Templates for Business Continuity and Disaster Recovery Planning are available in the Resource Library.

APPLICATION: This seems overwhelming; just take it one step at a time. What can you do to start the business continuity planning process today?

_____

_____

_____

_____

This lesson and the following lesson as well are adapted with permission from the work of Mike Semel, a business disaster preparedness consultant.

Disaster Recovery

Begin this lesson by reading the quote in the margin and reflecting on your own initial impressions about business continuity and disaster recovery planning. Do you find value in it or are you skeptical? How does the suggestion to consider it like an insurance policy re-frame your thinking?

_____

_____

Why plan? History demonstrates that if disaster strikes, businesses without plans are often doomed either to a much longer recovery process than those with plans or to going out of business. Although there are many new technology tools available to protect data and help businesses recover more quickly and simply than ever, the technology alone is insufficient. Having a plan helps to mediate the human component—getting you and your staff on the same page and ensuring that everyone knows exactly what to do. A basic written plan will help you execute your response at a time when you may be stunned, afraid, grieving, unable to think clearly, and may not even remember names or phone numbers.

Pick the choice below that demonstrates what should be first priority in case of a disaster.

    ❏ **Facilities**   ❏ **Operations**   ❏ **Safety**

Safety should always be considered of utmost importance. Employees must be taught that they should NEVER place themselves in danger for the company.

Natural Disasters. One area that you know well is the weather-related disasters that could uniquely affect your business because of your geographic location. These include tornadoes, hurricanes, earthquakes, fires, and flooding. You need to think through the impact such a disaster would have on your business, understand how to properly respond, educate your employees, and then run periodic drills.

Outages. We discussed briefly the impact that a power, phone, or internet outage could have on business continuity. Many plans fail because the planner assumed that all key employees will be available, power will be on, cell phones will work, deliveries can be received, and email and internet will be functioning. When that outage lasts for eight hours, one day, two days, a week…it becomes a disaster. How would you prepare for outages of different lengths?

Loss of Key Employee. One disaster that many businesses forget to plan for is the loss of a key employee due to sudden death or disability; going to work for your biggest competitor; going to work for your biggest client (whose revenue you may also lose); leaving when you have large projects looming; taking other employees with them. It is vitally important that for each essential job function in your company, you have identified a backup employee. Don't just think of losing your CEO or senior service

> _It initially may seem hard to justify putting all the resources into a solid business continuity disaster recovery plan. Lots of people ask me, 'where's the ROI in that?' But when you consider a BC/DR plan being similar to insurance, you realize there's great ROI. This very plan can be the difference between whether or not you even **have** a company._
>
> – Arlin Sorensen

person. What impact on your company would it have if you lost your accountant who knows the passwords and account numbers for the fiscal management of the company? Or your account manager who has relationships with many key clients and knows important information about those clients? Small businesses often only have one employee with a specific skill set. Your backup may work for another company, such as a similar business whose owner you know, and you have agreed that you will help each other in a critical emergency. A backup to your financial controller may be your accountant's office. Once you have identified a backup, make sure that he or she has adequate training and is resourced with necessary information, passwords, ability to access equipment or function-related areas of the facility, etc. This is an important impetus to make sure that no one is carrying valuable information only in their head.

Taking the time to plan and prepare your business and staff for disasters is not fun but is important and necessary. This has only scratched the surface, but we encourage you to utilize the resources found in the Resource Library, leverage the power of your peers, or engage professionals such as an attorney for more assistance in this area.

APPLICATION: The following checklist will help you to think through some key areas of BC/ DR planning. While not exhaustive, it provides guidelines to get you started. Have you prepared the following?

❏ Record of Insurance	❏ Off-Site Backup Solution
❏ Up-to-Date Employee Contact List	❏ Shelter-in-Place Inventory
❏ Facility Profile	❏ Off-Site Inventory
❏ Evacuation Procedures	❏ Passwords and Security Codes
❏ Media Policy	❏ Manual Work Order
❏ Alternate Site Identified	

Planning for Transition or Exit

ex·it strat·e·gy

/ noun /

1 Method by which a business owner plans to leave the business.

Begin this lesson by reading the quote in the sidebar and reflecting on this wisdom about legacy.

No matter how old you are today, it is inevitable that one day you will transition out of leading your company. You may desire to take your company public, retire and pass it along to a family member, or sell. Transition and exit planning are one key component of a business legacy plan. This lesson will briefly introduce these concepts at a high level.

Describe your own status in thinking through your exit strategy.

❑ **I've had an exit strategy since day one**   ❑ **In progress**

❑ **What do you mean I won't work forever?**   ❑ **Ready to start thinking**

Wherever you are in the process, thinking through how you can make a graceful, well-orchestrated, smooth, and hopefully profitable exit is worth the effort.

Evaluating Options

The first thing is to determine your mindset surrounding exit and transition as this will direct many other aspects of your plan.

Which fork in the road will you choose?

One option is to exit the business completely and either sell or close your doors. The second option is to have the business continue without you.

As you contemplate the possibilities, consider the people who will be impacted, which may include but are not limited to, yourself and your spouse, future generations of your family, staff, customers, family members, partners, and vendors. Obviously, your business legacy is closely tied into your personal legacy, so review your personal legacy plan before going further in this lesson.

Other Considerations: Control • Taxation Planning • Management • Asset Planning Long-Term Income and Value • Estate Planning • Transaction Planning

Feeling overwhelmed? You are in good company! Transition planning is a complex process and is not for the faint of heart. Do not try to create your exit strategy on your own. Involve your spouse, key employees, your peers, as well as the company Board of Directors, if you have one. Consider creating a team of advisors including your accountant and attorney, your insurance agent, banker, financial planner, and trusted business colleagues such as members of your peer group who have already been through the process. Having people external to your company who are vested in the success of the company share what they observe may be wise. The transition process can be emotional. Objective advisers can be a gift in helping to discern what is best for you personally, for your team, and for the company.

> *Leaders who fail the process of succession set their enterprises on a path to decline. Sometimes they wait too long, sometimes they never address the questions at all, sometimes they have bad luck and their chosen successor leaves or dies, sometimes they deliberately set their successor up for failure, and sometimes they just flat out pick badly. But however and whenever it happens, one of the most significant indicators of decline is the reallocation of power into the hands of leaders who fail.*
>
> *– Jim Collins*

If you see yourself pulling out, there are several options to consider:

- *Walk away* – Run it as a lifestyle business, taking the cash out of the business as it accumulates (being sure to save wisely along the way). Close the doors when you exit.

- *Sell it* – Sell it to others (employees, family, or to an outside source, etc.).

If you choose to keep or maintain the business, there are several different options:

- *Succeed it* – Pass the business down to a successor, often a family member.

- *Combine it* – Find another business to merge with.

- *Maintain it* – Hire someone to manage the business and keep it as a source of income.

Circle the option above that describes how you intend to get the value out of the company.

If you choose to have the business continue, succession planning is essential. Will you hire from inside or outside? If looking to make an internal promotion to replace you, begin identifying future leaders in each department and create personalized plans to help each leader develop the skills necessary to sustain the company.

Succession plans vary widely. Check the factors below which would cause plans to vary.

❏ **Type of Business**	❏ **Number of Owners**
❏ **Number of Leaders**	❏ **All of These Factors, and Many More**

Succession planning is about taking control of the inevitable and allows you to reduce the taxes paid, get the maximum value out of the business, leave it in the hands of chosen successors, and avoid business crisis. For the most successful transitions, plan for a transition period of three to five years or more. This allows for the selection of successor(s), training, adjustment, as well as a stock or money transfer.

How do I begin 'passing the torch?'

- Identify a successor. Either do an external search or identify a candidate internally.

- Bring the successor into your day-to-day activities by working side-by-side.

- Engage in systematic mentoring.

- Pass on some daily activities, starting with smaller projects or leadership responsibilities.

- Gradually release responsibility as you progress toward shifting larger projects and leadership responsibilities. The emphasis is on gradual. Don't dump all of your responsibilities on someone and run, expecting them to succeed. Model,

model, model. Then work together for a period on each responsibility. Transfer responsibility incrementally and observe, providing coaching or mentoring as needed. Plan the timing of your exit around their individual speed in capably taking over each area of the company. This means that you may need to alter your planned timeline midway through the process. Remember, no plan is set in stone; it's meant to serve as a guideline.

- Get out of the way!

Surprisingly, the most difficult part of the above is not succession planning or even the succession process itself…it's when the owner or leader is asked to let go of that last bit of control of the company and make his or her exit!

Since there are obviously far too many details to cover in a brief lesson, we will spend the remainder of this lesson preparing you to leave well no matter which exit strategy you select. Much of what we talk about will involve succession but can be applied to the other options as well.

The Logistics of Leaving the Business

The first step in preparing to leave your business is to determine your personal timetable.

How many years from now do you plan to exit/transition out of the daily operations of your company? How many years from now would you like to stop being an owner in this business? (Those answers may be the same or may be two different numbers.)

_____

Next, assess the roles and functions you currently serve within your company and determine what, if any, role you wish to retain in retirement.

Then with clear vision for how to exit, set SMART goals and create timetables for turning these functions over to your identified successor(s).

Communicate the plan and ensure that you have established clarity for how your exit will occur. Re-communicate and over-communicate to ensure you have clarity as you proceed through the process.

Finally, evaluate your progress as time goes by and make necessary adjustments to the plan.

Emotionally Preparing to Leave Successfully

The first mistake that many owners make is failing to plan their exit or to begin planning early enough to allow for an orderly, well-orchestrated transition. The second error that many owners make is underestimating the emotional toll leaving will take on them personally. As much energy as you put into planning the logistics of your transition, you need to spend at least as much if not more energy into preparing mentally to leave.

TIMELINE TO TRANSITION

Work backward to build a timeline with general dates and goals around financial preparation, staffing, transferring key relationships, etc.

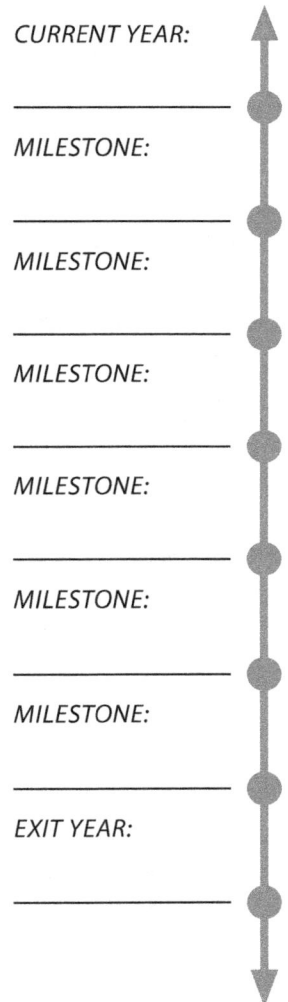

CURRENT YEAR:

_____

MILESTONE:

_____

MILESTONE:

_____

MILESTONE:

_____

MILESTONE:

_____

MILESTONE:

_____

MILESTONE:

_____

MILESTONE:

_____

EXIT YEAR:

_____

One reason it's hard to let go... your DNA as a successful entrepreneurial founder.

Do these resemble you?

- *Driven, used to relying on myself and taking personal responsibility for my decisions.*

- *Well-known entity in my community*

- *The 'go-to' person in my world, not accustomed to asking for help, assistance, or directions*

- *Spent most of career focused on one market for a long time and have developed a specialization and skills in that market, making it hard to transition to a new role.*

- *Personal identity is often wrapped up in the business—my name is on the door; I am strongly tied to my company's accomplishments.*

One key success factor is using preparation ahead of time to take emotion out of the transition. Creating a list of non-negotiables related to transition can be a useful exercise that lessens the impact of emotion when trying to make difficult decisions.

As you begin to pass along responsibilities, don't hover. Provide clear direction and expectations, but allow them the freedom to execute within those boundaries. Even more importantly, when they make mistakes (because they will) be there, not in the role of judge, but in the role of a mentor. Teach them to fail forward.

Your time will begin to free up as you shift more and more of your daily responsibilities to your successor. To prevent yourself from sticking your fingers back where they do not belong, commit to other activities. Enjoy this opportunity to do those things you always wanted to do, such as being an 'ambassador' for the company.

It is easy to become self-focused and have tunnel vision on how the exit is affecting you. Don't lose sight of the fact that you are not the only one being impacted; provide support for others (both your family and your team) and lead them through processing your exit as well.

When the time comes…LET. GO.

As mentioned earlier, the hardest part of the process often comes at the very end when you must make that final walk through the door of your company and fully entrust it to someone else. Unfortunately, many well-meaning business leaders end up sabotaging their own efforts.

Don't be like the gentleman depicted in a cartoon digging his fingernails into the carpet while being dragged from his office by his ankles. The caption says, "Of course, I could always stay on…in a purely advisory capacity…"

No one is ever ready to exit but with planning and careful execution, you can transition well and leave your company positioned for even greater things under the next generation of leaders. Now that's leaving a business legacy!

APPLICATION: Spend some time reflecting on your own exit. At the end looking back, how would you want to be able to describe the process of leaving your company? What steps will you take now to prepare to leave well?

_____

_____

_____

Business Value

Begin this lesson by reading the quote in the sidebar and reflecting on this wisdom about legacy.

Value creation should be a primary focus for any business entity in the for-profit sector. Creating value for clients ensures the sale of products and services. Creating shareholder value is vital for the long-term success of the company. As a business executive, shareholder value creation is one of your most important responsibilities.

From a simple financial perspective, value is created when a business's revenue exceeds its expenses, in other words, profit.

However, value creation is not narrowly measured on financial performance alone which can be achieved through short-term cost cutting. There are many factors that determine the value of a business, so it is vital to understand the factors that are valued in your segment or industry.

Value creation could be more broadly defined as making intentional and strategic investments to guarantee long-term competitiveness, growth, and viability.

The financial aspect of value creation deals with tangible assets, but it is equally important to develop intangible assets such as intellectual property, employee performance and loyalty, a strong brand, etc.

Value rests in perceived benefit. Whether you are attempting to provide goods and services customers find beneficial or to cultivate a company that others will want to buy, perception is reality in the case of value creation.

Determine Your Business Value Target (BVT)

In order to generate enough for the future, you need to answer some very important questions. If there are multiple partners or principals in the business, the answers must include everyone. This answer is related to the Personal Wealth Targets (PWTs) of the impacted individuals. Refer to the personal legacy chapter for more information on calculating your PWT.

What value does the business need to generate to meet the financial goals of the owners? (Don't forget to consider factors such as taxes, multiple owners, etc.)

_____

Your exit strategy will determine how that value is generated. For example, a Lifestyle Business does not have a large payout awaiting the owners at the end because they are taking value out of the company along the way. This requires careful planning and saving toward retirement.

A strategy to sell the company may require that the company grow or in some other way change to be desirable to a potential buyer.

> *To be successful, innovation is not just about value creation, but value capture.*
>
> *– Jay Samit*

Assessing Current Business Value and Predicting Future Business Value

The value of a small to medium-sized business varies based on many factors. Buyers may be looking to purchase a company in a certain geography to fill their footprint or to gain an established reputation in a market or an established customer base. They may be looking for employee skills or vendor relationships. Of course, strong and consistent financial performance over time is a crucial factor that potential buyers consider.

Do your homework within your industry and local market. Perhaps reach out to a consultant to get an official valuation estimate. There are no magic valuation tools, although they can be helpful in estimating value. A business is worth exactly what a willing buyer agrees to pay.

How much is the business worth today? _____

Determining the Gap

What is the gap between your Business Value Target (BVT) and the current value of the company?

How big is your business value gap?

BVT = $	_____
- Estimated current business value = $	_____
BUSINESS VALUE GAP = $	_____

What is your timeline to close the GAP?

Year you plan to exit:	_____
- Current year:	_____
TIMELINE GAP =	_____ years

How much do you need to grow the value of the business annually to meet your target according to your timeline?

BVT GAP = $	_____
÷ TIMELINE GAP =	_____ years
ANNUAL BUSINESS VALUE GROWTH GOAL = $	_____ per year

IN SUMMARY

- Our Business Value Target (BVT) is $ _____ .

- We have _____ years left to meet our target.

- We need to grow the value of the company annually by $ _____ .

Three Fallacies Surrounding Business Value

Many owners of companies consider the value they plan to extract from their business as part of the solution to fill the gap they have in their personal wealth (and rightly so).

However, unsuspecting owners are often surprised by three things:

1. **A failure to understand an essential truth:**

    HARD WORK DOES NOT EQUAL BUSINESS VALUE.

    They assume that working hard will generate an adequate BVT to span the gap.

    Buyers do not pay a handsome price for a company simply because the owner worked hard and was dedicated to their business for many years. Buyers do not pay for hard work, only true value.

2. **A failure to consider other factors that will erode the final amount they will individually receive from the company's sale. You need to ask yourself questions like the following:**

    a. Do you have partners? If so, how is the ownership split?

    b. What multiple of EBITDA do you expect to receive at time of transition? Value is often related to a multiple of the dollars of profit a company generates. In terms of business value, a dollar is not a just dollar but some multiple of it, so every dollar matters!

    c. How is the deal structured? How much of it is sure (cash up front) and how much is dependent (earn-out, etc)?

    d. What tax rate do you expect to pay on the proceeds of your business?

3. **A failure to do the math surrounding the connection between the BVT and PWT.** The final check seldom equates to the amount the owner originally anticipated. This is most concerning if business value is your sole solution for closing your personal wealth gap.

By doing the math and planning ahead, you can prepare well to grow the value of the business.

*APPLICATION: **So What? Now What?** You have ascertained the gap that exists in where the company is financially and where it needs to be. How will you close that gap? What is your business value creation strategy?*

_____

_____

_____

val·ue cre·a·tion

/ noun /

1 The performance of actions that increase the worth of goods, services, or even a business.

BUSINESSDICTIONARY.COM

> *Success is the peace of mind achieved when you know—in your heart—that you did your best at maximizing your potential according to your values. It has little to do with what others think of you.*
>
> – Darvin Raph

Create Your Business Legacy Plan

Begin your study by examining the diagram below.

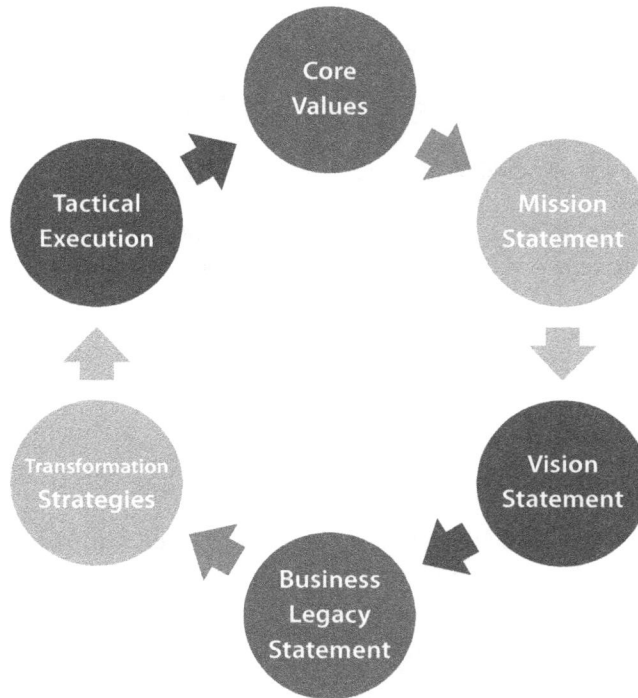

Hopefully, as you examined the diagram, you will notice that all of your hard work this week has paid off! Your legacy plan is almost complete.

In this lesson, we will simply put the pieces together.

This has been a challenging week. Which piece was hardest?

❏ Mission   ❏ Vision   ❏ Transformation Strategies

❏ Business Legacy Statement   ❏ Tactical Execution

Fill out the Business Legacy Plan which you see on the next page.

APPLICATION: Write down one good outcome that will come from the challenging work you have put in this week creating your legacy plan.

_____

_____

_____

Business Legacy Plan

Name   **Company**   **Year**

COMPANY MISSION	COMPANY VISION	COMPANY VALUES

Domains	Legacy Statement *What impact do you want your business to have in each domain? Write 2-3 sentences per domain.*	Transformation Strategies *How will you ignite transformation in this domain? Note a high-level strategy for each domain and target.*
Personal		
Business Partner(s)		
Employees		
Customers/Vendors		
Community		

Financial Targets		Exit Strategy	
Business Value Target	$	Exit Strategy	
Current Est. Value	$	Years to Exit	

TACTICAL EXECUTION

This document highlights areas or gaps where you may need to execute your legacy plan and for accountability in your peer group. Click the arrow next to each category to see suggested action items. The Influence column is to remind you to influence others in key roles in your company to do their part in planning for the company's legacy (business partners, key employees, etc.).

EXIT/SUCCESSION PLANNING

Update where you are on each of these considerations around exit. Have you considered...	YES	NO	ANYONE TO INFLUENCE?	NOTES
Identify what type of company you are (Lifestyle, Growth, Hypergrowth)				
Identify Exit Strategy				
Identify and Begin to Prepare a Successor (if applicable)				
Talent Retention Strategies				
Create an Exit/Succession Plan				
Phantom stock or deferred comp program				
Change of Control Agreement				
Children returning to work in the business				
Children taking over ownership				

LEGAL

Update where you are on each of these legal strategies.

Have you considered...	YES	NO	ANYONE TO INFLUENCE?	NOTES
Business Legal Structure (LLC, PS, S Corp)				
Shotgun Clause				
Buy/Sell Agreement • Partner withdrawal • Partner disability/death • Partner termination • Valuation Formula Agreement • Come along, drag along clause • Conflicting interest of stakeholders				

PLANNED GIVING

Update where you are on planning monetary giving.

Have you considered...	YES	NO	ANYONE TO INFLUENCE?	NOTES
Charitable Contributions				

TAXES

Update where you are on each of these tax considerations.

Have you considered...	YES	NO	ANYONE TO INFLUENCE?	NOTES
Income Tax Planning				

INSURANCE

Update where you are on each of these insurance considerations.

Have you considered…	YES	NO	ANYONE TO INFLUENCE?	NOTES
Risk Management: *Cyber/E&O*				
General Liability Insurance				
Life Insurance				
Disability Insurance				
Health Insurance				
Buy/Sell Insurance Funding				
Key Man Insurance				

CONTINGENCY

Update where you are on each of these considerations.

Have you considered…	YES	NO	ANYONE TO INFLUENCE?	NOTES
Business Continuity Plan • Strategy in event of death of a principal • Strategy in event of change in marital status • Partner distraction due to loss of family or family disability • Partner distraction due to care of parents/loss of parents				

Disaster Recovery Plan	
Hands that Give	

DIGITAL FOOTPRINT

Have you considered...	YES	NO	ANYONE TO INFLUENCE?	NOTES
Update where you are on managing and making plans to eradicate your digital footprint.				
Social media/blogs/pictures/data				

COMMUNICATION

Have you considered...	YES	NO	ANYONE TO INFLUENCE?	NOTES
Update where you are on each of these communication considerations.				
Stakeholders				
Who is vested in your success and lasting impact? Who needs to know about this legacy plan?				

ADVISORS

Have you considered...	YES	NO	ANYONE TO INFLUENCE?	NOTES
Update where you are on each of these relationships with experts in their field who can help you with your legacy.				
Bank/Broker/Financial Advisor				
Attorney				
CPA				
Insurance Agent				

Chapter 4: Notes

_____

_____

_____

_____

_____

_____

_____

_____

_____

_____

_____

_____

_____

_____

_____

_____

_____

_____

_____

_____

Business Plan

The Business Plan is an internally focused one-year plan making long and short-term strategy actionable. It ties to the business legacy plan and outlines how you will intentionally work toward your desired business legacy in the coming year.

It also takes more near-term business objectives around the functions of your business and prioritizes those to set goals.

A carefully thought out plan includes key financial targets, revenue projections, a budget, and plans for how you will resource each of your goals.

The business plan should outline goals for innovation or for improving internal operations. Additionally, it also contains goals important to sustaining the long-term vision of the organization such as developing a strong internal culture.

CHAPTER 5 LESSONS

Anchoring Your Company

Key Financial Targets

What's Important Now?

Create a Business Plan

Anchoring Your Company

Begin this lesson by reading the quote in the sidebar and reflecting on this wisdom.

In the legacy plan, we began with the end in mind. The business legacy statement you wrote in an earlier chapter paints a vision of a company led well. The vision is of the company a year before your exit. It describes what you want the impact of your leadership and of the company to be after you are no longer leading it.

Our focus shifts to the business plan in this chapter. We will review our legacy plan and then begin to lay out the path we will take. In this plan we will take the legacy plan's high-level vision and create goals. We will also incorporate more near-term business objectives.

Take a moment to look back at your business legacy plan.

Write your business legacy statement below.

_____

_____

Write your company mission statement here.

_____

_____

Write your company core values below.

1. _____   2. _____   3. _____

4. _____   5. _____

It is important that as you set off on this journey of mapping your business for the next year, you keep that compass of the company's core values firmly in hand so that you are mindful of them and checking every goal and action plan for alignment.

As you endeavor to plan your business year, you want to make sure you are looking through the lens of your mission, legacy statement, and core values. They are the anchor that will keep you from drifting toward things that seem exciting or urgent in the moment but that take your team away from what is important.

APPLICATION: Reflect on your company culture. How do your mission, vision, and values anchor your culture today? How would you strengthen this in the future?

_____

_____

Key Financial Targets

Begin this lesson by reading the quote in the sidebar and reflecting on this wisdom about business budgets.

Key financial targets should be set around revenue, profitability, and expenses. This informs the setting of goals and objectives but also must be connected to the Business Value Target.

What are you going to specifically do this year to grow the company's value?

_____

_____

Here are the things you need to consider as you generate your key financial targets for the year to come and fill out the key financial targets table on the business plan form:

REVENUE: The left-hand side of the financial targets are your revenue categories. Place revenue targets for each line item in the revenue column and total that column at the bottom with one total for both Products and Services.

GROSS MARGIN: The second column should contain your estimated gross margin percentage for each line item. At the bottom, estimate an overall blended gross margin percentage for your entire revenue mix.

EXPENSES: The right column should be your estimate of the percentage of total revenue across the three expense categories as well as the total expenses as a percentage of revenue.

EBITDA: EBITDA $ is the estimate of the actual dollars of profitability which can be used to calculate the current value of your business. EBITDA % is profitability divided by total revenue.

ADJUSTED EBITDA: ADJ EBITDA % is the percentage of profitability with appropriate adjustments made primarily based on owner salary compared to what the actual replacement cost would be to hire the roles filled from the outside. Utilize the adjustments from prior years as a guide to help you calculate your adjustment for this year.

BVT: Business Value Target can be copied from your business legacy plan.

Calculate the current value of the business by taking your current EBITDA $ and multiplying them by what you believe to be the likely industry multiple that will be applied. This typically falls between three to six.

YEARS TO EXIT: When do you anticipate stepping down from owning and leading the company? You can copy this from your business legacy plan. By dividing your gap between your BVT and current valuation by the number of years until exit, you will define the value you need to create annually to reach your target.

If you want creativity, take a zero off your budget. If you want sustainability, take off two zeros.

– Jaime Lerner

Minding the Gap

Let's apply the concept of legacy thinking or beginning with the end in mind. In our terms around financial metrics, this points to the two key numbers you determined in the chapters on personal legacy and business legacy:

- **Personal Wealth Target (PWT)** – What are you trying to accumulate in personal net worth before you no longer get a paycheck? What amount do you need to accumulate to sustain the lifestyle you want to live after leaving the workforce?

- **Business Value Target (BVT)** – How much value are you building into your company that will be extracted when you exit or extracted along the way and saved toward your BVT? Remember to consider partners, if you have them. The portion of BVT that is yours is then applied to the gap in PWT that most have while they are working.

Beginning with the end in mind financially, you can intentionally adjust some levers and manage toward those numbers while leading a business.

Your annual operating plan (business plan) should be a one-year step toward reaching your desired BVT. You close the gap between where you are and where you want to be one step at a time—year by year.

The length of time you have before extracting the value from your business plays a significant part in determining the rate at which you need to build company value. If you're exiting in a few years, it necessitates you drive value growth much more quickly than if you have 10 or more years before you plan to extract the value.

Here are five levers to consider as you look to plan goals around building business value in the year to come:

- **EBITDA $** are the profit dollars left after you pay all the expenses for the year. This is what a buyer really purchases when they acquire a company. EBITDA% is a good metric to track how efficient you are at generating that bottom line profit. But percentages don't pay bills, dollars do, so that is the critical number.

- **Gross Margin $** are the difference between your income and cost of goods (COGS). It is the margin on whatever you sell. These dollars pay the bills and eventually provide profit if there is money left over.

- **Multiple of service wages** is a metric that measures efficiency and utilization of service staff. A high portion of profitability comes from running an efficient and profitable service organization.

- **Multiple of sales wages** is a metric that measures the efficiency and effectiveness of the sales team. Cost of sales is often a key deterrent to profitability.

- **SGA** is the cost of sales, general expenses and administration. These get subtracted from Gross Margin to calculate EBITDA. Managing costs is one way to drive up the bottom line. However, managing costs is not possible if there isn't any gross margin. A wise CEO once said, "You can't cut your way to success." We can control costs, but this lever is only one small part of the solution to close your BVT gap.

There are plenty of other things that can be managed, but these five are key to planning how you will build value in the company.

Keep in mind that it takes time to make financial adjustments and correction. Starting with a plan sooner rather than later is wise.

Don't fall into the trap of assuming it will just work out. The Hundredfold Harvest team has the privilege of walking with companies through their journey of growth. It is very rare that members achieve their desired BVT without intentional planning and execution. Unfortunately, we more commonly see that those who haven't planned for their exit are not ready to exit when they wish to do so.

These people sometimes end up remaining longer in their business to intentionally build value so they can sell. Others realize they have owned a job and not a company and have to go on working well into the years they dreamed they would be retired. The demand for 60-70 year old entrepreneurs is pretty limited!

The good news is that you can achieve your financial legacy with a solid plan if you execute and give yourself adequate time.

Key financial targets should be set around revenue, profitability, and expenses. This informs the setting of goals and objectives. Tying these annual financial targets to the Business Value Target will help ensure that you are taking measured steps to build toward your desired financial legacy.

Turn to the Business Plan template at the end of this chapter and fill out the financial components on the first page:

1. The BVT and exit information at the bottom of the page.

1. The Key Financial Targets table in the center of the page.

> *The trouble with not having a goal is that you can spend your life running up and down the field and never score.*
>
> – Bill Copeland

What's Important Now?

Begin this lesson by reading the quote in the sidebar and reflecting on this wisdom about goal setting.

Determining Your Priorities

In this lesson, we are going to focus on prioritizing. There are many different demands on your time, so it is vital that you (using your core values as a guide) prioritize the areas where you want to devote time. Then you can act intentionally.

Look back at your Legacy Plan. Copy the transformation strategies on the lines below, one strategy per line.

Note the domain and then the strategy. There are five domains so you should have at least five strategies. If you have multiple strategies for a domain, give each strategy its own line. Draw additional boxes and lines as needed.

I'll do one as an example for you.   `1`   *Employees: Build a Leadership Team*

Ask yourself the question, "What's Important NOW?" Rank the transformation strategies in order of their priority for you currently.

Put a 1 in the box next to the strategy of highest importance, and an 8 next to the strategy of least importance currently.

There are no right or wrong answers! All the strategies remain options to pursue throughout the whole year. You are just prioritizing which to pursue first.

☐ _____

☐ _____

☐ _____

☐ _____

☐ _____

☐ _____

☐ _____

☐ _____

Now write your business objectives for the year to come on the lines below, one per line. How will you ignite success in your company's culture, finances, and people? Draw additional boxes and lines as needed.

Ask yourself the question, "What's Important NOW?" Rank the business objectives in order of their priority for you currently.

Put a 1 in the box next to the objective of highest importance, and an 8 next to the objective of least importance currently.

There are no right or wrong answers! All of the objectives remain options to pursue throughout the whole year. You are just prioritizing which to pursue first.

☐ _____
☐ _____
☐ _____
☐ _____
☐ _____
☐ _____
☐ _____
☐ _____

Setting Goals and Planning for Action

The next step is to look back at the top priorities of each list and combine them into one list. What's important NOW? You may create goals for four business objectives and just one transformation strategy. The combination will vary depending on your current needs and priorities. Over time ensure you don't allow the near-term (business objectives) to crowd out the long-term (transformation strategies). Both are important, but legacy items do not feel as urgent so can be overlooked. Work for a balance to keep walking toward your legacy. Remember that SMART goals are Specific, Measurable, Achievable, Relevant, and Time-Bound.

Here is an example goal based on the transformation strategy given above:

SMART Goal	Action Plan
Build a cross-functional leadership team of five people to start meeting in February.	• Determine who is on the team • Brainstorm meeting format with executive team • Plan dinner/team building kickoff • Establish leadership team meeting rhythm

SMART GOALS ARE:

SPECIFIC
They state what, by when, how, and by whom.

MEASURABLE
You can track and prove whether you met your goal.

ACHIEVABLE
They are possible given the parameters you have outlined.

RELEVANT
They align with your mission, vision, core values, and legacy plans.

TIME-BOUND
They define the time in which you will work to meet your goals and a deadline at which time you will assess your measurements and determine whether you have met your goal. These goals are not indefinite 'hopes' but steps that you commit to take in a given period of time.

Your turn. Take a combination of three to five of your top-ranked business objectives and transformation strategies listed above and write them as goals.

SMART Goal	Action Plan

Once you have written the goals, add an action plan of the three to five steps you need to attain each goal.

Breaking each down into bite-sized steps will help you to accomplish your goals. It will make what seems daunting feel more achievable, building your confidence and motivation to work toward that goal.

Building in Accountability

Setting the goal and planning for action are important, but goals are only effective if they are actually put into action. Accountability provides the needed guardrails that keep the team functioning and moving forward cohesively.

Designating someone who is accountable for each goal is vital. A team of people can be responsible to work on the goal, but only one person will be held accountable for its completion. This provides clarity about who is leading each initiative and who should field any concerns or questions.

Resourcing the goals you are pursuing is also important. Putting a dollar figure down to measure the financial cost is a good start. Remember to also include the time cost to your team so that one person is not over-leveraged and the goals are all able to be completed in the outlined timeframe.

The target date is the date when the goal will be completed.

APPLICATION: Read your goals and check them against the definition of SMART goals in the margin. Are your goals SMART? If not, revise them. Notice you are making your goals SMART-R by thinking ahead to the resources it will take to complete each goal successfully.

Create a Business Plan

Begin this lesson by reading the quote in the sidebar and reflecting on this wisdom.

Mission · Vision · Values · Strategies · Objectives · Goals · Plans

Hopefully, as you examine the diagram, you will notice that once again your hard work this week has been building. Your business plan is almost complete! In this lesson, you will simply put the pieces together.

Remember that the plan by itself is in no way a guarantee of success. Without consistent execution around the plan, it will simply remain a piece of paper that records a lot of important thinking and dreams.

The plan is not meant to be an annual plan that is created once and holds all the goals for the year. As with each of the plans, you need to review your business plan regularly. When a goal is accomplished, ask "What's Important Now?" and create a new goal around the transformation strategy or business objective of greatest importance.

You may want to create a scorecard for key areas of measurement, identify KPIs (Key Performance Indicators) to watch, evaluate and provide regular feedback to employees so they are aware of progress (or of progress that needs to be made), utilize the dates and benchmarks given with each goal, and communicate verbally and in writing about the status of your plan.

Creating the plan is the easy part. Now, go execute! You have planned your work; now, work your plan.

Business Plan

HUNDREDFOLD *Harvest*

Name

Company

Year

COMPANY MISSION	COMPANY VISION	COMPANY VALUES

KEY FINANCIAL TARGETS

PRODUCT	Revenue	GM%	EXPENSES	Expense	% of Revenue

SERVICE	Revenue	GM%

TOTAL EXPENSES/AS A % OF REVENUE

EBITDA %

EBITDA $/£/€
(Total Revenue x EBITDA %)

Business Value Target Strategy

TOTAL REV/OVERALL GM%		Current Value:	Gap:	Years to Exit:
BVT:				

TRANSFORMATION STRATEGIES (T)	BUSINESS OBJECTIVES (B)					
SMART Goal	**Action Plan**	**Accountability**				
		Who?	What Cost?	Status	Target Date	

Chapter 5: Notes

CHAPTER 6

Leadership Plan

Leadership is not for the faint of heart. It involves commitment, courage, a willingness to stay the course even through adversity, and the ability to cast a compelling vision. In this chapter, we will focus on creating a leadership plan.

The leadership plan is unique among the Four Plans because it spans both personal and business. So, it is tied to both legacy plans.

Just like the life plan and the business plan, the leadership plan is an annual plan. The legacy plans are vision documents, but the other three plans all contain goals for the year ahead.

Whether leading yourself, your family, or your team, leadership is primarily about influence.

CHAPTER 6 LESSONS

The Power of Influence

The Privilege of Influence

Which Hats Are You Wearing?

What's Important Now?

Accountable to Lead

A Culture of Accountability

Creating a Leadership Plan

The depth of leadership comes from the courage to put yourself after others, to sacrifice so that others succeed.

– Simon Sinek

The Power of Influence

Begin this lesson, by reading the quote in the sidebar and reflecting on this wisdom about leadership.

In this lesson we are going to explore your leadership journey. Who influenced you in the past? Who is currently leading you?

Let's begin with the past. Write down the names of several people who influenced you and impacted your life and/or career. These people could be people with whom you have personal contact or those whose influence was more removed, such as authors.

CHILDHOOD: _____

TEENS: _____

ADULTHOOD: _____

Reflect on these people you listed above and how they interacted with you and with others. How did they establish trust with you? What did their influence look like—was it gradual, direct or indirect, in person or through a medium such as their writing or radio show, etc?

_____

_____

Now let's transition to the present. All of us are constantly being influenced by others. There are several categories of leaders. For our purposes, we will consider the following three:

1. Thought Leaders share their ideas and shift paradigms

2. Inspirational Leaders motivate us to do or be more

3. Mentors care personally and spur us on to develop our full potential

First, we'll consider thought leaders whose podcasts and blogs we follow, books we read, or conferences we attend. It is possible to have too many voices speaking into your life at one time, especially in an era where it is hard to distinguish a genuine thought leader from the glut of self-styled 'experts' who seem expert mostly at promoting themselves on social media.

When you think about the number of thought leaders you are currently following, how would you assess that number?

The number of thought leaders I am currently following is:

     ❑ Too few   ❑ Just the right number   ❑ Too many

Explain. _____

Look at your podcast list, your blog feed, and your bookshelf. Write down the names of the thought leaders you follow.

_____

_____

True thought leadership comes as a by-product of experience, natural talent, research, or proven success. These people change the way we think about something and introduce original but relevant and important thought into a topical dialogue.

Consider the list of names you wrote in answer to the previous question. If you acknowledged that you currently follow too many thought leaders, circle your top two to three and consider taking a hiatus from following the rest. When the noise quiets, we focus and grow.

Inspirational leaders create strong emotional connections and motivate us to be excited about an idea or about the future. They move us to action.

Write down the names of inspirational leaders who are currently influencing your thoughts and moving you to action.

_____

_____

Who are your mentors? Mentors journey with us, watching our lives or career and making their wisdom available to us when we ask. You can have mentors across all different domains. You may have a professional mentor, a spiritual mentor, a marriage or parenting mentor, a mentor you are learning from within a hobby you enjoy, etc.

Write down the names of mentors who are currently influencing your thoughts and ways of behaving and leading.

_____

_____

APPLICATION: Wherever you are on your leadership journey, it is important for each of us to pause and acknowledge that we did not get to where we are today by ourselves. We have all been shaped and influenced by leaders. Whether it was our first leaders in the form of family members or teachers or those we currently learn from via books or podcast, leaders have affected each of our lives. Share a brief story about a moment of influence in your own life. Who influenced you? What was their impact on your life or career?

_____

_____

> _Leadership is not magnetic personality – that can just as well be a glib tongue. It's not 'making friends and influencing people' – that is flattery. Leadership is lifting a person's vision to high sights, the raising of a person's performance to a higher standard, the building of a personality beyond its normal limitations._
>
> – Peter Drucker

The Privilege of Influence

Begin this lesson by reading the quote in the sidebar and reflecting on this wisdom about leadership.

Leadership is not about a title or about a position. Leadership is influence. A leader is a person who remains close enough to relate to others but who is also out front, inspiring those following to keep going until everyone reaches the destination together.

Leadership is about integrity, honesty, and vulnerability. The interesting thing about being relatable is that when people are in close proximity to one another, there are no hidden flaws.

Leaders model for others what it means to be truly human. They create a circle of safety that frees others to be themselves as well and a culture where it is okay to admit mistakes as long as they are embraced as opportunities to learn and grow.

Leadership is a privilege; it is not a right. We are privileged to get to walk with others and to influence them. The true test of leadership is whether or not anyone is following. Leaders have followers. Leaders are among the privileged for they are influencers.

This lesson will challenge us to look at ways our actions serve as a conduit to invest our experience, knowledge, and talent in developing those we lead.

Whom do you lead? Think across your roles in your company, your family, as a volunteer. Think about those you mentor. It could be individuals or a team. Note their names and roles below.

For example, you might write "Sales Team, John – marketing manager, Louise – daughter, Chris – volunteer in XYZ community organization."

_____

_____

Since there are no perfect people, that means each person we lead has a gap between where they are currently performing and their potential. (It also means you have a gap between your own current leadership performance and your potential to steward your influence for the benefit of those you lead…but we'll tackle your leadership gaps in the next lesson.)

Identifying the gap for those you lead begins by defining success for each role. If possible, including some objective standards or metrics to measure assists in providing clarity.

Defining Success

Many of us do not provide clarity for those we lead. They feel pushed back and forth by the winds of our mood. One day they do something, and we praise them. The next day they do the exact same thing, and because we are in a bad mood, we find fault with what they have done. Their job feels like a cycle of 'read the boss's mood and adjust accordingly to try and please them.'

It is important to define success in a way that is objective and not subjective to how we are feeling in the moment. We want to empower our people with a clear definition of success, so they know what is expected of them in their role, and both the leader and the follower can agree how they are doing regarding that expectation.

> *People value integrity, but they follow clarity.*
>
> *– pastor and leadership author Andy Stanley*

How Do We Define Success?

The answer is to sit down and think about what excellence looks like in that role. Separate the role from the person who is currently filling it. If you had the ideal person in that role, describe their performance. How would they perform their duties personally? How would they interact with the team? With clients or customers? What expectations do you have of them as a professional in their role?

Each company will define success slightly differently. Write your definition of success and then ask someone who is a high performer in the role you are defining to provide feedback. Allow them to ask questions to make things clearer. Ask them if there is anything you added that they would question or anything that you neglected to add that would be important to include.

Here is an example of definitions provided by sales SME Steve Riat. These frameworks outline possible categories that should be considered when defining success for a sales manager or a sales rep.

Defining Success for Sales Roles	
Sales Manager	**Sales Reps**
• Team Quota Attainment • Team Development (Meeting Cadence, Training, etc.) • Goal Accomplishment (Tool Integration, Quota, Marketing, and Such) • Forecasting (For Executive Team) • Personal Development for Manager (Leadership Training, Life Plan, and More)	• Individual Quota Attainment • Appointments • Close % (of Quotes) • Renewals • Sales Activities - (Entering Them in a CRM, Follow Ups and Marketing Activities, etc.) • Personal Growth - (Skills Growth, Legacy and Life Plan, etc.)

To define success for a sales position, you would take these categories Steve provided and customize the definition with the detailed expectations for that role within your company. For example, you would put an actual expected close percentage in the definition of success for a sales rep.

If you are a member of a peer group, this is a great opportunity to leverage your peer group. Ask another member what their definition of success would be for that position. Expectations will vary by company, but the majority of the categories included should be common to all companies. Suggestions for defining success for service and finance roles are available in the Resource Library.

Look at the list of people you lead. List each role in the first column of the table. Then define success for the role itself—try to separate them from the role. Then write a short appraisal of that person's current performance. Finally, note any gap that you can help each person you lead to close by investing in their personal and leadership development.

Role	What does success look like?	How is this person performing against that measure of success?	Gap between performance and success

For each individual or team where you have identified a gap, create a development plan of how you will work with that person to grow them and close that gap in the year to come.

Person/Team	SMART Goal	Action Plan

APPLICATION: Spend time reflecting on the difference between a reservoir and a conduit. Why is it important for leaders to be conduits? How can leaders teach those who follow them to also be willing servant leaders who generously and graciously give away their presence, their knowledge, and experience to develop others?

Which Hats Are You Wearing?

Begin this lesson by reading the quote in the sidebar and reflecting on this wisdom about leadership.

Before you can lead with vision and clarity, you must first achieve vision and clarity by examining the roles you fill on any given day. It is okay to wear multiple 'hats.' Being in the small to medium-sized business (SMB) space often necessitates several hats as we do many of the same functions as large and enterprise businesses but with a skeletal crew. However, it is not effective to concurrently wear multiple hats. When you are acting as the owner and making decisions around driving shareholder value, you should not also be worrying about daily management questions and putting out fires. It is important to set aside dedicated time to fully 'wear the hat' of each role you are expected to fill.

> **This will be a fun exercise. Jot down the number of roles you estimate you fill within your company and then list them.**

_____

_____

If you are like many leaders, you struggle to get through each day's long Task List, let alone move the organization forward strategically.

Which 'hats' do you wear on a regular basis? Check all that apply.

- ❏ CEO
- ❏ President/GM
- ❏ Hire/Fire
- ❏ Sales Manager
- ❏ Accountant
- ❏ Service Manager
- ❏ Marketing
- ❏ Technician
- ❏ Facilities
- ❏ Customer Service
- ❏ Salesperson

And most likely several that aren't listed. So many hats. Only 168 hours a week, and only a small portion of those are supposed to be allotted to work.

Use the circle to create a pie chart that shows how much time you spend wearing each hat. Divide the pie into sections, then write the name of the role and the percentage of time you spend wearing that hat. Note the frequency you spend time in that role. Is it weekly, quarterly, annually?

lead•er•ship

/ noun /

1 The position or function of a leader, a person who guides or directs a group.

2 Ability to lead.

3 An act or instance of leading; guidance; direction. (Leadership, 2012)

Synonyms: foresight, administration, initiative

The Five Leadership Roles

The 'hats' that you checked (and many more that were not even listed) all fall under one of five leadership roles. In providing structure, clarity, and guidance for your company, it is important to be aware of which hats you wear and which one you are wearing at any given time.

Ownership	• Focuses on Stakeholder Value • Long-Term Driver is Business Value
Leadership	• Focuses on Strategy • Long-Term Driver is Growth
Management	• Focuses on Operations • Long-Term Driver is Performance
Team	• Focuses on Tactics and People • Long-Term Driver is Productivity
Individual	• Focuses on Job • Long-Term Driver is Happiness

Now refer to the previous question. Map the hats you checked to the leadership roles listed below to help you begin to delineate your roles.

Ownership _____

Leadership _____

Management _____

Team _____

Individual _____

There could be a whole curriculum on the leadership roles alone. For the sake of this lesson on leadership planning, this introductory awareness will suffice.

Mapping the Team

Create a team map showing each team member's leadership roles and the time they spend filling each role. Here's an example chart:

ROLE	TEAM MEMBERS				
	Bill	Jenny	Dan	Steve	Susan
Owner	25%		5%		5%
Leader	75%	15%	25%	50%	25%
Manager		75%	20%	25%	50%
Teammate		5%			10%
Individual		5%	50%	25%	10%

Write each team member's name at the top of a column. Then continue down the column and write the percentage of time they spend functioning in each leadership role.

ROLE	TEAM MEMBERS				
Owner					
Leader					
Manager					
Teammate					
Individual					

Spend some time analyzing and discussing this chart with your team. This will give you a clear view of how you are currently leveraging your team and ways in which some roles may be neglected.

Here are some questions you might discuss as a leadership team:

- Assess each person's capacity. Anyone overwhelmed? Underutilized?

- Is there anything a team member is currently doing that should be delegated to someone else to free him/her up to focus more on individual Highest and Best Use (HABU)?

- Do you have meeting rhythms for each of the layers of leadership?

- Assess the health of each layer of leadership. How faithfully are you maintaining your meeting rhythms? Is there any area that eclipses other areas in terms of time and focus? Is there any role that needs more intentional attention?

Remember: The real value of this leadership roles exercise comes from its ability to help generate conversations within your team.

APPLICATION: Jot a few notes about any surprises that you discovered doing the Five Hats and Leadership Role Team Mapping exercise. What actions will you take because of this lesson?

> *Good leaders pursue more than the bottom line. They see character as their primary means of influence. Our lasting legacy will come more from who we are than from what we have done.*
>
> *– Wayne Stiles*

LIFE DOMAINS

BUSINESS DOMAINS

LEADERSHIP ROLES
Which hats are you wearing?

What's Important Now?

Begin this lesson by reading the quote in the sidebar and reflecting on this wisdom about leaders.

In this chapter, we have practiced others-first leadership by focusing on how we will invest in those we lead. Now we will turn and tackle a hard challenge: looking in the mirror. Self-leadership involves influencing yourself to achieve your goals and vision.

A wise leader once said, "The toughest meeting I have each day is with the person I see in the mirror."

Effective self-leadership goes hand in hand with having a long-term perspective. Talented leaders realize that their consistency across time is important. They are not only looking for quick wins but more importantly for sustained, effective growth.

Great leaders are also self-reflective. They assess the domains of their life and work against principles and goals. They are aware of their strengths and weaknesses and examine their behavior to grow as humans.

Most importantly, people who lead themselves well are humble. They are forgetful of themselves and focused on others. They recognize that they are still learning and growing and embrace the journey.

How effective are you currently at leading yourself? Put an X in the appropriate spot on the continuum.

INEFFECTIVE ⟵————————————⟶ *EFFECTIVE*

Identifying and Closing a Leadership Gap

In the lesson on the Privilege of Influence, we discussed the reality that there is no such thing as a perfect person. We noted that since none of the people you lead are perfect, they will have gaps in their performance.

You are also a person. Thus, you are imperfect and will have gaps in how you perform. Remember that the leadership plan is unique among the Four Plans because it spans both personal and business.

Look at the margin and review the different domains. What is a way that you need to step up and lead yourself in order to close a gap in your leadership?

A leadership gap sometimes points to a behavior you need to START doing such as spending individual time with each of your top performers, being present with your family at the dinner table instead of being distracted by your phone, or taking time daily to reflect and journal.

The quarterly scorecards available to all as part of the Quarterly Performance Dashboard are useful to identify a leadership gap. Look at your Spouse, Life-Work Tension, Manager, or Legacy scorecard. Pick one item where you have received a low score for several quarters. That is likely a leadership gap.

Write a Leadership Gap you would like to close here:

_____

Maturing Out of Muscle and Feel

'Muscle and Feel' is a term we use to describe something we rely on our intuition or capabilities to accomplish.

A muscle and feel task is often something we should STOP doing. For different reasons, we know we 'should' delegate that task, automate it, or put a process in place to make the task more efficient. Yet, we have felt compelled to continue muscling and feeling that task forward.

Before you create a plan, take a moment to pause and ask yourself, "WHY am I doing it?"

There may be a legitimate concern or reason why you have remained involved. For example, if you micromanage the financial reporting process because you have concerns about the accountant's accuracy, then you need to either have a conversation with your accountant or replace him or her before you let go of your vigilant oversight of the finances.

Many times, however, we muscle and feel something for one of two less legitimate reasons: either we haven't slowed down to take the time to delegate it properly or we have held on to something simply because we enjoy it. We enjoy the task itself, or we enjoy playing the role of 'Superman' or 'Superwoman' and being needed by the company or team in that way.

However, if you continue to muscle and feel things that you should either let go or allow to become a more mature process, you will be the blocker to your company's growth.

Begin by analyzing the different things you do. Then ask yourself a few questions about each task to identify something you are muscling and feeling:

1. **What is the opportunity cost of continuing to do this task myself?** In other words, what am I not able to do because I am using my time to do this?

2. **Am I fulfilling my HABU (Highest and Best Use)?** If not, what can I get off my plate, so I can do the things that only someone in my position or with my strengths can do for our company?

3. **Is there a place where I am 'bottlenecking' the company?** If you are unsure, ask your team _"Where do I stick my fingers into something and slow things down?"_ They'll tell you!

4. **What am I currently doing that I should create a process for or delegate to someone else?**

> _Success happens when we realize that leadership doesn't start and stop – it is how we live day by day and moment by moment._
>
> – Arlin Sorensen

Effective Leaders

1. *Don't try to be right; they try to be clear.*

2. *Give their best ideas away and empower others to own them.*

3. *Bring opportunity out of difficulty.*

4. *Create more leaders.*

5. *Truly believe they can make a difference.*

Identify a task where you currently operate out of muscle and feel:

_____

A quick note on delegation. Many people fall into one of two extremes when they delegate. They either micromanage, or 'dump and run,' meaning give someone the task but not provide the ongoing support to make sure they can assume that duty successfully. Successful delegation means that you have taught someone else to do the task so well that they can go beyond you and improve how it was done.

Setting Goals and Planning for Action

You have determined a leadership gap and one thing that you are muscling and feeling. The next step is to write a SMART goal for each. Remember that SMART goals are Specific, Measurable, Achievable, Relevant, and Time-Bound. Here is an example goal based on a leadership gap in the personal domain:

SMART Goal	Action Plan
Meet bi-weekly with an executive coach starting in February to work on growing in self-awareness.	• Engage coach • Schedule coaching calls

Your turn. Take the leadership gap and task you are muscling and feeling listed above and write a SMART goal for each.

The goals could involve the behavior you are trying to address directly. They may also revolve around a book you will read, a skill you will learn or sharpen, a class or conference you will attend, etc.

Category	SMART Goal	Action Plan
Leadership Gap:		
Something I Muscle & Feel:		

Once you have written the goals, add an action plan of the three to five steps you need to do to achieve each goal.

Breaking each down into bite-sized steps will help you to accomplish your goals. It will make what seems daunting feel more attainable, building your confidence and motivation to work toward that goal.

Accountable to Lead

Begin this lesson by reading the quote in the sidebar and reflecting on this wisdom about the importance of accountability.

Our team defines accountability uniquely. We often say that accountability is not watching someone set a goal and then standing back and waiting for them to fail or not act so that you can criticize them. Rather, accountability is about taking ownership of the outcome AND of your impact on others in the process of accomplishing your goals.

Reflect on this definition of accountability. Do you agree or disagree? How would that definition play out practically with your team? Family? Community? As you allow others to hold you accountable?

_____

_____

There is an aspect of accountability that is closely linked to personal responsibility—accountability is about taking ownership for your own actions and for how your actions affect those around you. Our view of accountability also has a communal nature. It is a sharing of the burden of a task. It involves caring so much about another person that you personally invest in their success.

Does this sound familiar? Hopefully, for those who are clients or members of our peer groups, it reminds you of many of the aspects of being part of a peer group or receiving coaching and consulting services from our organization. The concept of accountability is woven throughout our culture.

A Culture of Accountability

Check the things you view as being vital to building a culture of accountability.

❑ Clarity ❑ Company Retreat ❑ Trust ❑ Data

Clarity and trust are both essential building blocks if you are setting out to create an accountable organizational culture. So is data. DATA?!? Yes. Keep reading for an explanation.

> *It is not only what we do, but also what we do not do, for which we are accountable.*
>
> – Molière

ac·count·a·ble

/ noun /

1 Subject to the obligation to report, explain, or justify something; responsible; answerable.

Synonyms: responsible, liable

It is hard to force people to take accountability for their actions when they lack access to information. In order to be able to hold your staff fully accountable for their performance, it is important that you identify numbers and metrics that drive your success AND that you dashboard those numbers.

You must ensure that your staff not only sees them frequently but understands those measures and how their job can move each lever. The adage is true that what gets measured, tracked, over-communicated, and rewarded gets done.

Clarity around roles and responsibilities as well as goal assignments will go a long way. One reason the need for accountability is emphasized is because of the far too common scenario in which many employees are unsure of what they are accountable for in the first place.

An accountable culture sets goals for ALL staff, not just leaders, managers, and sales staff. Each staff member should know what is expected of him or her. They need to know what success means for their role.

Read the following statements. Then indicate if they are true of your company.	True of my company	Not yet
We have a written job description for every position in our company.	❑	❑
My staff members are all aware of their job responsibilities, goals, and accountabilities.	❑	❑
We set goals for ALL our staff (even admin staff).	❑	❑

Drive clarity around 'what by when' and also around core values. Communicate expectations not only around performance but also around values. Values need to be constantly top of mind for everyone in the company —in everything our company does, we act this way. These values are who we are. We live out of our identity as part of ABC Company.

How have you made your corporate values part of the culture of your company? If they are not part of your culture, what step could you take to begin to keep your values in front of your employees and customers?

_____

_____

Clarity of direction will also help with motivation as teammates realize that their execution on a particular task does matter. They comprehend their progress on that task will be checked at regular intervals, not so they can be criticized but in order that you can help them with any roadblocks. You want to trust but verify, checking *in with* each direct report to make sure things are progressing well without leaving them feeling like you were checking *up on* them.

Trust is the second building block for accountability. If your team has built trust, each member is free to focus on his or her part of the goal, knowing that the entire team is executing and laboring with excellence to achieve their goals.

Trust provides the support needed to take risks and invites creativity. It allows you to be proactive instead of reactive, since you will not have to worry about unforeseen crises among team members. It is important that a culture of safety be cultivated and trust be exercised from top to bottom in an organization to have a true culture of accountability.

Think of a scenario in your own leadership past when the culture lacked trust and you were blindsided and responded in a way that was reactive rather than proactive. How might being proactive have changed the outcome of the situation?

_____

_____

Finally, to build a culture of accountability you need to reward success in a way that is meaningful to each individual. You also need to deal decisively with mediocrity. Failing to deal quickly with deficient performance sends a message to the rest of the team that you are not serious about accountability and erodes culture.

Barriers to Accountability

While some people are naturally disciplined and accountable, others resist accountability. Their natural tendency is to justify and explain away their responsibility if something goes wrong.

As a leader, you can do a lot to cultivate an environment where people operate at a high level of personal responsibility. This type of environment is a place where people feel safe to admit a mistake and have learned how to fail forward. There is clarity not only around their own tasks but around other team members' roles and tasks as well (including those at the highest levels of leadership).

There is a shared direction and vision along with strong motivation to go there together. A culture of accountability is a culture of mutual caring and service, where employees serve one another first and well so that they can more effectively serve clients as a unified team.

In this Barriers to Accountability section, which of the descriptions of a culture where people operate at a higher level of responsibility describe your company currently? Underline each one. Which do you hope will describe your company in the future? Double underline and star each one.

Characteristics of an Accountable Culture

- *Staff members know what success means for their roles.*

- *Employees live out of the identity of who they are as team members at your company.*

- *People understand how their execution moves levers and helps the company move ahead.*

- *Each team member feels free to be creative and take risks.*

- *Employees trust everyone is working with excellence.*

- *A healthy culture allows people to be proactive.*

- *People feel safe to make a mistake.*

- *Employees understand other team members' roles as well as their own.*

- *Success is celebrated.*

- *Mediocrity is dealt with decisively.*

What About When Goals Are Missed?

It is inevitable that at some point, someone on your team will fail to execute. We encourage you and your managers to regularly visit with your direct reports to find out when someone is stuck at the point they are most in need of assistance. Train your managers to ask, "What can I do to help?"

Still, there will be times when a goal is not met, and there is nothing you can do. When that happens, how can you lead well? Use it as an opportunity to teach.

Put on your coach's hat and ask the following three questions:

1. **How did you contribute to this situation?**

2. **Looking back, was there a point when you saw a problem? If so, when? What could you have done at that point to get back on track?**

3. **What will you do differently in the future, so this doesn't happen again?**

This lesson will end with a true story witnessed at a consulting engagement at one of our clients, who shall remain nameless. It is the story of four people named Everybody, Somebody, Anybody, and Nobody.

There was an important job to be done and Everybody was asked to do it. Everybody was sure Somebody would do it. Anybody could have done it, but Nobody did it.

Somebody got angry about that because it was Everybody's job. Everybody thought Anybody could do it, but Nobody realized that Everybody wouldn't do it.

It ended up that Everybody blamed Somebody when Nobody did what Anybody could have done.

APPLICATION: Share about a time when you or someone else missed achieving a goal. How did you handle it? What would it look like to use it as an opportunity to teach?

_____

_____

_____

_____

A Culture of Accountability

Begin this lesson by reading the quote in the sidebar and reflecting on this wisdom about leadership.

The Leadership Plan is all about creating a culture of leadership starting at the top. It is about the company leadership creating a shared vision and setting the example of what it means to lead. It is about leading yourself first and growing into a leader worth following.

This plan is also about building the people who will build the business. It is what will create a sustainable and successful organization. Too many have taken this plan lightly. After all, if we are the boss or the parent, we don't necessarily feel the need to be accountable to anyone. That is a privilege of our position, right?

Not exactly. While it may feel good in some respects, unaccountability and a lack of leadership is a formula for status quo at best and complete failure at worse.

Accountability must begin at the top and filter down to the rest of the team or family or whatever group of people you are leading. Without a culture of accountability, you will struggle to build a sustainable entity.

If you as a leader do not take personal responsibility for your actions and decisions, how can you expect those who are supposed to be following you to do so? Here are some examples of a culture that lacks accountability:

- Setting goals that are unlikely to be met

- Expecting others not to meet their goals

- Not following through on action items

- Having a recurring cycle of denial, blame, and excuses

- Failing to communicate consistently and clearly

Accountable leaders are solution-focused and are confident in their own ability to eventually solve any problem. They accept responsibility and refuse to accept excuses. If they are unable to meet a deadline, need help, or have confusion about a task, they say so. By being real about their own struggles, they give those following them the freedom to be real as well.

Accountable leaders attack problems, not people. They stay up to date on the metrics, provide accurate and timely feedback to employees, and use those agreed upon standards and deadlines to hold people accountable for their performance. They celebrate success and have a low tolerance for mediocrity or a lack of personal responsibility.

Finally, accountable leaders never lose sight of their personal core values or of corporate values and take care to align their every action with those values.

How accountable is your culture? Put an X in the appropriate spot on the continuum.

UNACCOUNTABLE ⟵——————————————————⟶ *ACCOUNTABLE*

According to Executive Coach Hardin Byars, "A culture of accountability is one where we do not have to hold people accountable. It is a culture where accountability comes from within and is not imposed from the outside. We don't want to hold people accountable; we want people to BE accountable."

Hardin suggests four ways to cultivate and reinforce a strong culture:

- Anchor everything to the Mission, Vision, and Values.

- Manage by celebration. Look for positive examples of the culture and reinforce them.

- Look for negative variations and use them as opportunities to teach.

- Practice radical candor where you care personally and challenge directly.

On the leadership plan form, there is a column titled Status and one titled Target Date. These allow your accountability partners to help you succeed.

In the status column, you 'stoplight' your pacing and progress.

- **Green** indicates you are on pace to achieve your goal by the target date

- **Yellow** indicates you are slightly off pace; there is a possibility you may not achieve your goal by the target date.

- **Red** indicates either you are stalled due to a roadblock or that you will not achieve your goal by the target date.

The target date column should be filled in with the date by which you commit to complete the goal.

APPLICATION: List one thing you can do to either create or strengthen a culture of accountability within your company.

_____

_____

_____

_____

Creating a Leadership Plan

Begin this lesson by reading the quote in the sidebar and reflecting on this wisdom about leadership.

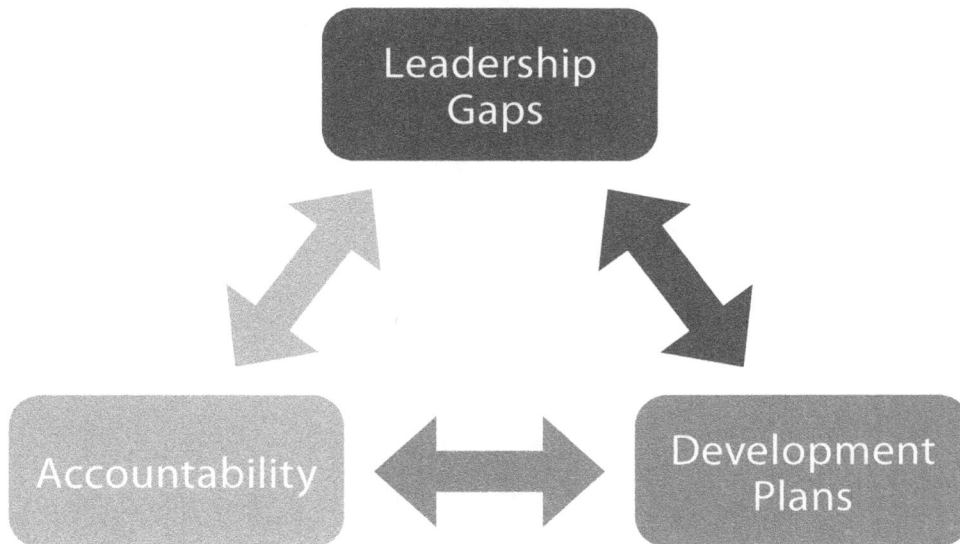

Beyond the horizon of time is a changed world, very different from today's world. Some people see beyond that horizon and into the future. They open our eyes and lift our spirits. They build trust and strengthen our relationships. They stand firm against the winds of resistance and give us the courage to continue the quest. We call these people leaders.

– James M. Kouzes and Barry Z. Posner

Hopefully, as you examined the diagram, you will notice that your work has paid off! Your leadership plan is almost complete. In this lesson, we will simply put the pieces together.

The real measure of a leader is that they actually *have* followers, people who are coming behind them because they believe in the direction they are being led and not just because they are paid or obligated.

Leaders don't just lead at work. They begin with the person in the mirror, and it carries over to home, to community, and to every other aspect of life. It doesn't mean you always have to be in charge. But it does mean you lead by example.

Sometimes that is in how we follow or support the one up front. It can be stepping up in the discussion or refocusing the group on what matters.

Start now and really consider how you will lead. Be accountable. This plan can be a critical success factor in your business, your marriage, and your home as you learn to look in the mirror, be humble and aware of your own leadership gaps, and then work with others to help them grow and develop.

Don't take this one lightly. Do it well! You owe it to yourself and to those you lead. Influence is a powerful privilege. You have been poured into by others. Now, choose to steward that gift by exercising your privilege to develop others.

Leadership Plan

Name **Company** **Year**

PERSONAL MISSION	PERSONAL LEGACY STATEMENT	PERSONAL VALUES

LEADING MYSELF
How am I igniting transformation in my leadership?

	SMART GOAL	ACTION PLAN	STATUS	TARGET DATE
My Leadership Gap • What leadership gap do you commit to work to close this year?		•		
Muscle & Feel • What are you currently using "Muscle & Feel" that you need to lead yourself to mature/transition?		•		

Building My Team

COMPANY MISSION	COMPANY VALUES

Identifying & Closing the Gap

Think about those you lead or invest in as a Go Giver. What are the gaps you need to close within each function or role?

PERSON OR TEAM YOU LEAD/MENTOR		
ROLE OR FUNCTION		
DEFINE SUCCESS FOR THIS ROLE (INCLUDE APPLICABLE METRICS TO MEASURE)		
CURRENT PERFORMANCE IN THIS ROLE		
GAP BETWEEN CURRENT PERFORMANCE AND SUCCESS		

DEVELOPMENT PLAN (PERSON'S NAME/TEAM NAME)	SMART GOAL	ACTION PLAN	STATUS	TARGET DATE
		.		
		.		
		.		

Chapter 6: Notes

_____

_____

_____

_____

_____

_____

_____

_____

_____

_____

_____

_____

_____

_____

_____

_____

_____

_____

_____

_____

_____

Establishing Rhythms

Take some time to celebrate! You have developed a vision plan for your personal and business legacy. You have also created life, leadership, and business plans with goals that serve as a one-year step to walk toward that legacy.

You've accomplished some important things, thoughtfully considered ways to invest in your family and staff, and envisioned your desired future direction. Now the most important steps are ahead.

With the planning complete, you can begin to execute those plans and turn them into more than just a piece of paper, a few months of demanding thinking and clever ideas.

As Thomas Edison said, "Vision without execution is hallucination."

In this chapter, we are going to raise the likelihood of you being successful in executing on your plans. We will establish rhythms—rhythms of review, of accountability, of execution—all intentionally crafted to help you accomplish your goals in every area.

Map Your Plans

Begin this lesson by reading the quote in the sidebar and reflecting on this wisdom about the importance of prioritizing goals.

In this lesson, you are going to map your plans, looking across all of the plans and determining which tasks you will do daily, weekly, monthly, and yearly to execute on your goals.

If possible, photocopy your plan worksheets or tab the pages as you will be doing a lot of flipping back and forth to those pages.

Take a moment to familiarize yourself with the Execution Map of Plans on the following page. We recommend that you take each plan individually and follow the row across, putting the action steps for each goal in the appropriate box.

Here are a few questions you can ask yourself about each action step as you assess the appropriate frequency of task execution:

- Is this a task that is performed one time or is it a recurring task?

- How often is the task performed?

- Is this an independent task or a collaborative task that involves colleagues? If so, with whom will you work to accomplish this item?

Tip: If it is a collaborative task, take the time to send out a meeting invite to your colleague and schedule time to work on the action item together. That will help to ensure you do not leave it to the last minute and keep the goal top of mind for both of you.

Once you have the chart filled in, either photocopy it and place it somewhere that you can see it or transfer the information to your calendar so that your tasks are scheduled.

A journey of a thousand miles begins with one step. Mapping your progress ensures you don't miss any of the key steps along the path and can consistently execute your way to fulfilling your goals in each area.

Execution Map of Plans

Plan	Yearly	Quarterly	Monthly	Weekly	Daily
Personal Legacy					
Life					
Leadership					
Business					
Business Legacy					

Communicate with Stakeholders

The secret of getting ahead is getting started. The secret of getting started is breaking your complex overwhelming tasks into small manageable tasks, and then starting with the first one.

– Mark Twain

Begin this lesson by reading the quote in the sidebar and reflecting on this wisdom about the importance of doing each next thing.

Stakeholders are those people who have invested in you and/or your company, have a personal interest in who you are and in who you are becoming, and because of that investment of time, interest, and energy, have the most at stake. In other words, stakeholders are those with whom you are in closest relationship such as a spouse, children, other family members, close friends, etc. Business stakeholders include partners, key employees, trusted business colleagues, professional advisors such as your attorney and CPA.

Make a list of your stakeholders (both business and personal):

Business Stakeholders	Personal Stakeholders

Why Communicate My Plans?

On a basic level, communicating personal plans such as your life, leadership, and personal legacy plan with stakeholders is *an invitation to a deeper relationship.* Whenever you invite others into your dreams and goals, you invite them into relationships. It opens the door for others to take an active role in your life and to help you achieve those goals.

From the standpoint of your business and business legacy plans, **it is common sense.** Even if you have the best strategic plan ever created, it is unlikely to be successful unless it is clearly communicated to those tasked with implementing it: your colleagues and employees. Including key stakeholders who are vested in your success such as vendors, distributors, your attorney, accountant, etc. is also important.

Too often planning is done at the top and then never shared beyond the executive and leadership teams. Planning must be communicated and re-communicated until there is clarity across all departments and job roles in the organization. Every single employee needs to understand why his or her job matters to the company's vision as well as how what they do day-to-day can 'move levers' that will drive the team toward achieving their goals.

Leaders often take it for granted that their staff understands the plan because they all sat through a staff meeting where the CEO spent ten minutes showing the presentation from the leadership team's recent strategic planning meeting. If they need a refresher, the vision/mission/values are on the website, right?

If the employees cannot execute the strategic plan, the leaders need to take responsibility for not communicating well. It is the leader's responsibility not only to communicate clearly but to communicate frequently and to ensure understanding.

Finally, communicating your plans is *an invitation to accountability.* This will be the subject of a future lesson, so that's all that will be said on the topic here, but it is important to mention.

How Should I Communicate?

You need to weave your strategic plans into the fabric of the culture of your company. Every employee should be able to articulate your mission, vision, and values when asked. A customer should be able to see what you stand for because they are getting the same cultural experience no matter with which employee they interact. Employees should know where the organization is headed and how their role fits with that vision.

Communicate, re-communicate, over communicate to achieve clarity across the organization. Once you have communicated your plans, remember to provide regular and relevant feedback to let each person know how they are making an impact in helping the team reach the collective goals.

You need to communicate:

> 1. Clearly　　　2. Often　　　3. Simply　　　4. Providing Feedback

A presentation at a single staff meeting, a binder on a shelf, and posting your mission/vision/values on your website is not enough. Planning is important but is not sufficient in and of itself. Communicating to clarity is also a key component to executing well and achieving your strategic vision.

APPLICATION: Reflect on your communication practices. Which of the four ways of communicating do you do best? Which do you most need to improve? How will you improve?

_____

_____

_____

_____

_____

> *Give me six hours to chop down a tree, and I will spend the first four sharpening the axe.*
>
> – Abraham Lincoln

Aligning the Organization

Begin this lesson by reading the quote in the sidebar and reflecting on this wisdom about the importance of organizational health.

Global Clarity Precedes Personal Clarity

Picture your organization as a pyramid. At the top of the pyramid is what the organization is trying to accomplish at the corporate level.

Corporate clarity then cascades down the pyramid until every person has clarity within their individual role. As individual people make decisions, ideally they make those decisions in alignment with the long-term objectives of the company.

In order to provide that clarity, employees must understand how decisions are made within the organization. Then each can apply that understanding to a specific decision within their role and answer questions from their manager like those posed here:

- Given what we are trying to accomplish, what do you think you should do?

- What options are on and off the table?

- Of the options on the table, which option advances us toward the goals we are trying to achieve?

- Are there any that conflict with those goals?

- Are there any that are simply a waste of time?

Executive Coach Hardin Byars utilized a powerful tool called 5 Question Clarity that measures alignment between the employees and organization. (Do they answer the five questions in the same way you would answer them for that person in their position?)

It also provides employees with clarity at a personal level. It is effective with employees who understand the organization's core values and norms of behaviors.

Before using 5 Question Clarity with your team, sit down and write out your answers to the following questions: What is the organization trying to accomplish? How do you define success at the corporate level? At the business unit level? For each position that directly reports to you? How will you reward your team if you succeed?

_____

_____

Using 5 Question Clarity

5 Question Clarity consists of five questions that apply to every employee, irrespective of position within the company.

Each manager should fill out the five questions for each employee who directly reports to them.

Then ask each employee to personally answer these five questions:

1. **What are we trying to accomplish?** (What does success look like for the company this year?)

2. **Where do I fit in?** (How does what I do impact the mission? How does it impact the bottom line?)

3. **What are my boundaries and resources?** (Boundaries are areas in which I can make a unilaterial decision.)

4. **When we are successful, what's in it for me?** (Not just money...sense of contribution, purpose, etc.)

5. **How am I doing?** (What am I doing well? What are areas where I can grow? Are there any responsibilities or expectations I am not fulfilling?)

Comparing each employee's answers with their manager's answers will show where there is alignment. If you find you do not have alignment, you can use this tool to have conversations that align the employee with the organization's direction and expectations.

When the leadership of the company and the employee both answer the questions in the same way, alignment has been achieved.

This exercise facilitates important conversations with employees. Asking these questions is not only about understanding what they currently know but also assessing how they are thinking. Is this employee thinking about the future and the implications of where they are heading?

Building Your Team

Every road leads somewhere. We can ask questions to help employees think through where their current path will take them. This helps them, and the company as a whole, both end up at their desired destination.

5 Question Clarity is one tool or exercise that is useful in developing people. The most important thing is to have open and regular rhythms of communication.

Clarity is the essence of leadership. The higher the degree of alignment, the more effective your organization will be.

Developing people is not about perfection; it's about progress. If you feel hesitant to start a rhythm of investing in your people and having coaching conversations, don't feel anxious. Just start. Step in and begin building the people who will build your business.

APPLICATION: Try using 5 Question Clarity with one of your direct reports. Reflect on the experience. What was hard? What was rewarding? What did you learn?

If you could get all the people in an organization rowing in the same direction, you could dominate any industry, in any market, against any competition, at any time.
– Patrick Lencioni

Rhythms of Accountability

If you could kick the person in the pants who is responsible for most of your trouble, you wouldn't sit for a month.

– Theodore Roosevelt

Begin this lesson by reading the quote in the sidebar and reflecting on this wisdom about accountability.

Part of the process of accountability is setting up rhythms of reporting.

There are two types of accountability.

- **Personal accountability** is taking responsibility for your own self-leadership.

- **Organizational accountability** involves the team providing a second layer that should parallel and support your personal accountability.

Personal Accountability

Personal accountability begins by having a meeting with the person in the mirror. As leaders, we own accountability for our actions and the completion of our goals. Unfortunately, many of us are not that disciplined and are quick to make excuses or blame others.

There is value in having one or two people to whom you are accountable. However, occasionally we assume the person we have asked to hold us accountable will be coming to us.

Instead, your responsibility is to regularly report to them on your goals and progress so that they do not have to chase you down to hold you accountable.

Part of being accountable to someone else is making it easy for them to do so by transparently and consistently reporting your progress (or lack of progress). This includes scheduling regular check-ins.

Organizational Accountability

Meetings and a strategic planning system are the main tool for reporting around organizational accountability.

Additionally, each manager having regular one-on-ones with their team members is important. These can occur on a monthly or weekly rhythm but should be frequent enough to provide the clarity needed for the team member to be effective in their role and to know if they are on track to achieve the goals assigned to them.

One-on-ones can take different formats. An example of effective questions a manager can ask during a one-on-one include the following:

- How can I help you?

- What's going well this week? What wins can we celebrate?

- Where are you stuck? What roadblocks can I remove for you?

- What resources do you need to do your job?

Organizational accountability and the measures around it should provide input into the performance review process as well as be a motivator to stay focused and deliver results.

APPLICATION: Think about your personal and organizational accountability. How can you improve your rhythms of reporting to make both more effective?

_____

_____

_____

_____

> If you had to identify,
> in one word, the reason
> why the human race
> has not achieved, and
> never will achieve, its full
> potential, that word would
> be 'meetings.'
>
> – Dave Berry

Meetings

Begin this lesson by reading the quote in the sidebar and laughing at this funny quote about meetings.

Do you share Dave Barry's perception of meetings? Many people do. They view meetings as a waste of time and dread company meetings. While many companies' meetings would perhaps fit the above description, your company's meetings can be different. If used rightly, meetings can be an integral tool to focus the staff, bring clarity around vision, and keep the team executing on the important rather than getting sidetracked by the urgent things constantly clamoring for their attention.

Respond to the paragraph above. On a scale of 1 to 10 (1 being our meetings are just "noise," 10 being our meetings are valuable tools and an integral part of our culture), rate your company's current meeting structure.

      Our Meetings: 1 2 3 4 5 6 7 8 9 10

If your meetings were to become a thing of the past, would employees cheer or feel that the company had lost something important? Explain your answer.

_____

_____

The key to having effective meetings is getting into a rhythm. Consistent scheduling, consistent agendas, and consistent expectations go a long way in transforming your meetings from being something employees endure to something they anticipate. Effective meetings help both the team and individuals function more effectively.

What are you feeling as you read about this unique perspective on meetings?

❑ **Skeptical — no way this will work**   ❑ **Anticipation — can't wait to try**

❑ **Cynical — been there, done that**   ❑ **Affirmed — we already do this**

Successful companies have an established rhythm of meetings, and they consistently stick to that routine, giving their employees a structure and clarity of expectations. We highly recommend that you buy the book *Mastering the Rockefeller Habits* by Verne Harnish. In his book, Harnish makes a shocking statement: "Growing companies should have more meetings, not less" (Harnish, 2006). The more you've got going on, the more important it is for you to bring people together and consistently communicate to drive clarity and execution around what is important.

Here is the meeting rhythm that Harnish advocates (modified somewhat) and that many growing members have found to be an instrumental part of their success:

Meeting Rhythm		Time	Focus	Attendees
Annually	Measure progress in the previous year, create a forward-looking, proactive strategic plan, and set new goals.	2 days	Strategy	Leadership and subset of employees
Quarterly	Measure progress toward specific goals. Deep dive into several goals. List top three accomplishments and challenges. Adjust as needed.	½ day	Strategy	Management or Leadership Team
Monthly	Departmental QBRs: Review financials, prior month performance; talk about goals for the next month; work through challenges/ questions.	1-2 hours	Learning	Executive Leadership Team
Weekly	Begin with a Core Values moment (How did you see one of our values lived out this week?), share good news, the numbers, customer and employee feedback, focus on a single issue.	30-60 minutes	Team Building, Clarity	Entire Staff
Daily	What's up?, Daily Measures, Where are you stuck?	5-15 minutes	Problem Solving	Departmental

Many follow Harnish's lead in calling daily meetings 'huddles.' This name gives a good picture of what these meetings are meant to be: quick, tactical meetings intended to drive things forward by dealing with daily challenges and communicating clarity across a team.

Remember: The key to successful meetings is consistency, consistency, consistency.

APPLICATION: Which of the meetings are you going to try? What benefits do you see from having a rhythm of meetings?

meet·ing

/ noun /

1 An assembly or conference of persons for a specific purpose. (Meeting, 2012)

Synonyms: gathering, assembly

Establish Rhythms of Review

Begin this lesson by reading the quote in the sidebar and reflecting on this wisdom about the importance of reviewing your plans.

You have worked hard throughout this workbook. Now that the plans are written, though, don't just put your notebook up on a shelf and check off the 'planning' box on your to-do list.

Think of a voyage at sea. Just because a captain charts a perfect course does not mean he can put away his maps, sit back, and just let the ship sail itself.

Constantly changing conditions require him to vigilantly monitor his ship's path. His stance is watchful, aware of things that might blow the ship off course.

He allows his sailors to do their jobs, having trained them well, but is always ready with a word of encouragement or guidance since he knows that each one's individual effort greatly impacts the success of the whole voyage.

The captain is ready to step up to the helm at a moment's notice to steer the ship should it veer to the right or left. If he's not seen on deck or at the helm, you may find him in his cabin checking the charts he knows so well. He regularly reviews the ship's desired course and makes sure the ship travels in the right direction to reach that destination.

He doesn't stop until the ship has made it safely to port.

What valuable behaviors of a business leader would parallel those of a ship captain? List them below.

_____

_____

Your business and life do not have an 'Autopilot' option. In the same way that the ship captain does not view the voyage as a chance to take a pleasure cruise, you should not either. He did not sit back and let his sailors work according to his clear charts of how the voyage should go; in the same way your active role in the business is vital and indispensable.

Your overarching view of the business includes the history, status, and future vision. You also have a deep understanding of the systematic way every role works together for the success of the company. The combination of these two factors allows you the unique ability to guide and keep the business on course to achieve your goals.

(These each apply even more so to your ability to keep your life and personal legacy on your desired course! No one knows you like you. And no one can live your life but you.)

The graphic in the margin shows a path followed by successful leaders. They begin by taking time to **think**. It is hard to provide leadership when a leader is always pouring out and not taking any time to refresh his or her own thoughts. Stepping back to reflect on where things are today and refresh your vision of where you would like to be in the future is an important discipline.

The second step is to **plan**. Hopefully, you have seen the value in that step. President Eisenhower said, "Plans are worthless, but planning is everything." It is planning that can open our eyes to potential mistakes to avoid and opportunities on which to capitalize.

Planning forces us to stop long enough to think through and visualize where we are going. It gets us out of 'fire drill' mode where we are simply reacting to the emergencies that arise day-to-day. It provides an opportunity to think strategically and prepare proactively for the future.

Planning brings people together and can create synergy as you give others visibility into your dreams and goals. It's not the plans but the process of planning that brings the greatest value.

After they plan, successful leaders **do**. They execute. They are disciplined and systematically take small step after small step to achieve their goals.

Finally, successful leaders **review**. Rather than allowing their plans to simply become an afterthought or another binder to clutter up an already full shelf, they treat plans as living documents.

They are constantly measuring their actual performance and that of their staff against their plans and core values to make sure they align and are advancing the company toward their envisioned future.

We encourage you, at a minimum, to review each plan at least quarterly. Monthly is preferable. It can be a quick process where you just look through each area briefly, note the strategic objectives, and assess what has been accomplished and what is yet to be done.

It helps prevent things from being overlooked and a last minute scramble to accomplish forgotten goals before the strategic planning session for the following year.

APPLICATION: Create a schedule of review that will work best for you. Will you review plans monthly? Quarterly? Bi-annually? Yearly?

_____

_____

_____

_____

In each area, ask yourself:

- *What have I done this month/quarter to move the company forward in this strategic area?*

- *What should I focus on next month to help us keep moving in the right direction?*

- *Where do we need to realign?*

- *Where do we need to put additional effort going forward?*

- *Where have we made good progress, and I need to lead the staff in celebrating?*

Chapter 7: Notes

_____

_____

_____

_____

_____

_____

_____

_____

_____

_____

_____

_____

_____

_____

_____

_____

_____

_____

_____

_____

_____

_____

Self-Leadership

The secret of great leaders is that they lead from the inside out.

They have first become self-aware which leads to greater accountability and understanding of others.

Great leaders are influencers who can intentionally and positively impact the thinking, feeling, and behaviors of a team to pull people together and achieve shared goals. However, before they became effective at leading a team, they first learned how to lead themselves.

No one ever arrives at a point of complete mastery in any area of leadership, but especially in self-leadership. People are people everywhere. You, as part of humanity, will always be imperfect and will make mistakes. Great leaders are those who learn from mistakes and use that knowledge to grow and mentor others.

This concluding chapter is designed to encourage you and help you to identify habits enabling you to lead yourself and then others.

These habits will bring you not to a place of perfection but to a place of personal excellence as you learn to live consistently, to be oriented toward personal growth, and when you do fail—because you will—to fail forward.

CHAPTER 8 LESSONS

Time Management

Communication and Email

Personalities

Continual Reflection and Learning

Live Your Plans

Time Management

Begin this lesson by reading the chapter introduction and reflecting on the topic of Self-Leadership.

What can fly or crawl but can't be stopped from passing? You had a slight clue if you looked at the title of today's lesson. The answer, of course, is time.

In an earlier lesson we talked about some of the great equalizers in life, things that are experienced equally by all of humanity, regardless of one's age, gender, location, or income. Check the boxes that were mentioned.

❏ **Time**   ❏ **Education**   ❏ **Taxes**   ❏ **Death**

Time is one of the most precious gifts we are given. Each person receives 168 hours a week, no more and no less. Regardless of how awful a day at the office has been, you can with good probability look forward to receiving a new 24 hours to steward the next day.

Time is common to all of us; what differentiates you from another person is the choice of how you use your time.

Without over-analyzing, look at the statements below and choose the one (or two) that describe your view of time.

❏ **Time is a resource to manage**   ❏ **Time is never enough**

❏ **Time is a precious gift**   ❏ **Time is something to invest**

Entrepreneur Arlin Sorensen shares about a shift in his perspective that occurred in January of 2005. He was out shoveling snow on a routine winter day when he felt a tightness in his chest. He went to the doctor who decided to do a stress test. Arlin was stopped in the middle of his stress test, and a cardiac catheterization was scheduled at the city hospital.

When they went to do surgery, the plan was to put in a couple of stents; however, they found the situation to be more serious than anticipated. What began as a routine winter weekend found Arlin undergoing quadruple bypass surgery.

That event serves as a key marker in his life as each day and each breath became something for which to be grateful. Arlin now considers each day he is alive a blessed day because he gets to wake up and enjoy his family and colleagues.

Have you ever experienced a similar shift in your view of time? If so, briefly describe the situation and how it impacted your perspective.

_____

_____

How we view and understand time, as well as the importance we place on it, greatly impacts how we choose to use our time. If you view time as never being sufficient or as something that is rapidly running out, you will spend your life feeling frantic and trying to stuff every moment full of busy activity. Many people with this view arrive at mid-life and have a 'crisis' because they feel like their life is slipping away.

The opposite view of time is that time is a gift and something to be invested. If you hold this view, instead of being focused solely on the quantity of time you have, you will spend your life looking for ways to increase the quality of your time. When you arrive at mid-life, you don't panic because you have not been thinking of minutes as units that are depleting; you have been focused on investing time. The person with this perspective can rest in the knowledge that time appreciates when it is invested.

We were created with limits and boundaries—with 365 days in a year and 24 hours in a day. We must live within the boundaries we were given and choose how we will use the time.

Think back to a typical week. Using the time tracking tool found at the end of this lesson, write down everything you did from the moment you woke up until you went to sleep in 30-minute increments.

Refer to the time grid you made. Have you been using time wisely—investing it carefully to get the greatest return? Have you been using time unwisely— squandering it on things that don't matter and won't last? Have you been thoughtless in how you use your time, not giving thought to the fact that time is finite and that you choose how you use it?

☐ **Wise**   ☐ **Unwise**   ☐ **Thoughtless**

Remember, the first step to self-leadership is self-awareness.

If you discovered that you have been unwise or thoughtless in your use of time, be thankful. No, that is not a typo.

It is only in becoming aware, that you can begin to lead yourself toward better stewardship of your time.

If you see that you have been using your time wisely, be thankful. And remember that no one arrives at perfection. Use the rest of this lesson to see if there is something you can learn to be even wiser in how you invest your moments.

> *For every minute you are angry, you lose sixty seconds of happiness.*
>
> – Ralph Waldo Emerson

Making the Most of Your Time

You have most likely heard the well-known story in which a professor stands before his class with a jar and puts some big rocks in, asking his class, "Is it full now?"

The jar appears to be full and the class answers, "Yes." The professor proceeds to put smaller rocks, sand, and finally water in the jar, pausing between the addition of each new material to ask the class if the jar is full.

The moral of the story is not that you can always squeeze one more thing into your schedule. Rather, to manage your time effectively and invest it wisely, you should begin with your big rocks first.

Begin by clarifying your priorities, both at home and in life. You have already done this with your Life Plan.

What would it look like to think of your priorities for your role in your company? What are the 'big rocks' that you need to put in first? It could be making time for annual strategic planning and quarterly reviews of each plan. It could be intentional time spent coaching your people, focused around their personal and career growth. Perhaps it is focusing on driving shareholder value or building relationships in the community or in your peer group. What are some 'time wasters,' things that urgently clamor for your attention (and usually get it), but are not adding value to your life or your company (such as TV, interruptions, procrastination, poor email/communication habits, not reviewing the day or planning for the next, etc.)?

Fill in the chart below to identify your 'big rocks' and some 'time wasters' both in life and in your job. Look back to pages 45-46 to review the priorities you identified for your life.

Managing my Time			
My Life		*My Job*	
Big Rocks	**Time Wasters**	**Big Rocks**	**Time Wasters**

What a great start! You have clearly defined your priorities. Now you have a filter by which to measure tasks and opportunities. If it is a time waster or is not an investment of time that will bring a good return, just say "No." You only get to use each hour once, and then it's gone. Use your time for what matters; don't waste your time on anything else.

You have been entrusted with enough time to make the lasting impact you desire. You just need to steward the time you've been given well. You have already given great thought to how to live by your priorities in your personal life. Here are some general principles that will help you to make the most of your time on the job:

- **Start Right.** Plan your week and your day. In the appendix, you will find a form that is helpful in planning your week. You choose your three Big Rocks, or tasks that are important to accomplish that week. Then you break each rock down into tasks. Finally, you equally allocate the subtasks across the week (three per day) so that if you do the three things you have written down for each day, you will have accomplished your big rocks at the end of the week.

- **End Right.** End each day by reviewing. Take five minutes to look back at your day and specifically at your three Big Rock priorities. Ask "What worked well? What didn't work? What could work better?" Celebrate small wins and ask for help with struggles. Look ahead to tomorrow and review your three priorities for the next day. Finally, take a moment to capture any thoughts you want to remember so you can be present at home once you leave work.

- **Have and Follow a Communication Policy.** We will look at this in depth in the next lesson.

- **Keep the Big Rocks in View.** Do what needs to be done. Don't get caught up in taking care of little tasks or allow yourself to be sidetracked by interruptions. Invest your time in the areas where it will make the greatest impact.

- **Schedule Office Hours.** Set aside time to be available for helping your team. Expect them to come prepared and to follow the Communication Policy.

- **Use Meetings Effectively.** We look at this in depth in another lesson.

- **Manage Your Email.** We will look at this in depth in the next lesson.

- **Refresh Yourself.** You don't need to have a 'martyr mentality' with respect to your work. It is important for your health to take time to refresh yourself daily, weekly, quarterly, and annually. (See guidelines in sidebar)

APPLICATION: Which of the above principles would make the biggest impact on your efficiency and work life?

DAILY:

Start and End Right. Set breaks (many doctors recommend at least five minutes up walking around every 90 minutes).

WEEKLY:

Set aside a block of time to think and review.

QUARTERLY:

Set aside at least a half day for planning.

ANNUALLY:

Set aside at least two days for strategic planning and one day for renewing your other plans. Take your vacation time wisely.

TIME USE WORKSHEET (Part 1)

- Assume we spend 8 hours per day sleeping and 4 hours on tasks such as eating, household chores, personal grooming, etc.
- Our goal is to account for 12 hours per day or 364 hours per month.
- Identify and summarize regular activities.

Time	M	T	W	Th	F	Sat	Sun
6:00 – 6:30							
6:30 – 7:00							
7:00 – 7:30							
7:30 – 8:00							
8:00 – 8:30							
8:30 – 9:00							
9:00 – 9:30							
9:30 – 10:00							
10:00 – 10:30							
10:30 – 11:00							
11:00 – 11:30							
11:30 – Noon							
Noon – 12:30							
12:30 – 1:00							
1:00 – 1:30							
1:30 – 2:00							
2:00 – 2:30							
2:30 – 3:00							
3:00 – 3:30							
3:30 – 4:00							
4:00 – 4:30							
4:30 – 5:00							
5:00 – 5:30							
5:30 – 6:00							
6:00 – 6:30							
6:30 – 7:00							
7:00 – 7:30							
7:30 – 8:00							
8:00 – 8:30							
8:30 – 9:00							

TIME USE WORKSHEET (Part 2)

- Using the activities you recorded in Part 1, classify them by domain in the table below.
- Note the frequency per month you engage in each activity.
- For hours per month, when an activity is consistent weekly, multiply by 4.33 weeks per month.

Domain	Activity	Hours per Week	Frequency per Month	Hours per month
For Example: PERSONAL	Exercise (swimming)	3	Weekly	12.99
PERSONAL				
FAMILY				
CAREER				
SPIRITUAL				
COMMUNITY				

Self-discipline is the ability to make yourself do something you don't necessarily want to do, to get a result you would really like to have.

– Andy Andrews

Communication and Email

Begin this lesson by reading the quote in the sidebar and reflecting on this wisdom about self-discipline.

One of the biggest time traps is inefficiency in communication, especially email. Most people don't manage their email; it manages them!

If you are like many, you spend a lot of your day answering questions for your team and wading through a backlog of email.

In this lesson, we are going to examine some simple policies to help you gain back time that you are wasting due to not having efficient communication and email habits in place.

Describe a typical scenario in which a team member has a question or problem and comes to you seeking advice and/or approval. How does the staff member present his/her request? How do you respond?

_____

_____

Did the team member come to you with a question? Did you answer it? That may be the source of some of your frustration and inefficiency.

If you set yourself up as the 'wise one in the corner office' and continually solve your team's problems, they will continue to come to you with their questions and issues; and you will have interruptions and a backlog at your door.

You have probably heard the adage, "Give a man a fish, and he'll eat for a day. Teach a man to fish, and he'll eat for a lifetime."

There is value in having a communication policy that outlines how to communicate. Part of growing leaders is teaching them how to think critically and to solve their own problems, within the boundaries of the company's mission, vision, values, and strategic plan.

To read a sample communication policy, refer to the appendix.

React to the communication policy in the appendix. Would this work in your company? Which parts would work well? How could you adapt or modify it to fit your culture and needs?

_____

_____

One of the biggest ways people waste time at work is on email.

How much time, on average, do you spend each day on email? _____

How many items are currently in yourinbox? _____

If you haven't ever tracked the number of minutes you spend on email, keep track for a day. It's usually a shocking amount of time.

How do you manage your email?

1. **Realize your email is often urgent but is frequently not important.** Refuse to let email derail your day and take you down rabbit trails. Stick to your priorities and work at accomplishing your Big Rocks.

2. **Schedule time to read and respond to email.** Turn off email alerts. Don't check your email first thing when you get to the office. Close your email program unless it is during the scheduled time when you are supposed to be working on email.

3. **Change your attitude.** Instead of viewing email as an overwhelming avalanche of information that you just try to stay ahead of, make up your mind that you will get to the point each day where you have a small number of emails in your inbox.

4. **Use the Four D's.** See the sidebar for elaboration on the Four D's.

5. **Configure your email account.** Use the tools. Create rules each time you get a junk mail message, blocking the sender. Create bracketed folders for emails that you are [CC]'d on, for those that you are informed about [FYI], for newsletters and things you like to [Read], and for items on which your staff needs [Approval]. Teach your staff to use [Approval] in front of subject lines of items where they have an issue and are proposing a solution. Then create rules to route messages to those folders and out of your inbox. When it is the scheduled time to check your email, look at the [Approval] folder first. Then go through your inbox and use the Four D's. Be disciplined! You can get your inbox to a manageable number of emails each day.

6. **Have an email standard.** The To line is reserved for the person who is accountable. (Only one name on that line in most cases.) If a name appears in the CC line, it means FYI (read when you have time). Make it your practice to respond within 48 hours, or in the case of approvals or decisions, within 24 hours. When you are home or on vacation, make up your mind to be present to the people whose company you are enjoying. Email can await your return. Don't let it erode your attention to those you love and value. Either commit to not check email at all or set a schedule and respond to emails only once or twice a day.

APPLICATION: Reflect on today's lesson. What do you already do well? What do you need to improve? Which idea/tip will you implement right away?

Four D's of Email Management

1. *Delete:* Get rid of junk mail (and block sender).

2. *Do:* If you can act on it right then, do so.

3. *Delegate:* Forward to the person you are delegating to; ensure you provide clarity on the task you are delegating.

4. *Defer:* Schedule time to deal with the email later and copy the email into the notes section of the appointment before deleting.

Personalities

Begin this lesson by reading the quote in the sidebar and reflecting on this wisdom about teamwork.

As you learned earlier in the week, self-leadership begins with self-awareness. That is true in many areas but especially that of personality. If you do not understand your own personality and the way that you are wired, it is difficult to understand others' personalities and your interaction with them.

Have you ever taken a personality profile? Describe what you learned about your personality.

_____

_____

_____

There are many personality profiling tools available that provide valid results. We often use GiANT's 5 Voices model because of its ease of use and application to effective communication. Whether you use the 16 Personalities, the Big 5, DISC, or any number of personality models available, we encourage you to consider how a personality style assessment can be used as a tool to build your team.

Many peer group members who have used a personality assessment tool within their own companies have found it to be helpful in providing a common, easily remembered language for the staff to use when interacting.

Your understanding of personality will impact every area of your leadership including how you hire, how you communicate, and how you deal with conflict.

For example, while it may be easy for a 'life of the party' extravert to hire other people who are outgoing since they are so much fun to have around, a wise leader understands that having a diverse set of personalities on the leadership team will benefit the organization as each one's strengths are different.

Take a moment and create a 'DNA map' of the different personality types in your organization. What different personality types and mixes do you have and in what positions do they serve?

_____

_____

_____

Relating well to one another begins with awareness. When you are aware of another person's personality type, you can use that knowledge to help you communicate and interact more successfully with that person.

Here are some ideas from peer group member companies who have utilized a personality profile to help their team to communicate.

- Team members each put their personality into the status of their instant messaging tool. This heightens the awareness of other team members to know how to approach different people in a style they understand.

- Several team members chose to display a humorous sign or picture in their offices to communicate their personality type to those coming for a face-to-face chat. The example in the margin is just one of many creative displays employees have created.

- There's a column in the company phone directory listing each employee's personality type. A cue sheet reminding team members of each personality is provided and kept near the phone.

- At a recent team meeting, employees from various locations were asked to perform skits highlighting a negative communication incident and a positive interaction among people with different personalities.

When the awareness of personalities permeates a team, it impacts a culture and makes the work environment more pleasant for all involved. Relationships involve work; if you want strong relationships, you have to cultivate them.

By choosing to consider how another person is wired and putting energy into understanding their perspective, you are valuing them as a colleague and investing in strengthening your relationship.

APPLICATION: Reflect on today's lesson on personalities. What value do you see in growing in your self-awareness and leading your team to better understand the different personalities that make up your company?

_____

_____

_____

_____

_____

---

per·son·al·i·ty

/ noun /

1 The essence of a person's character revealed in predictable patterns of inclination and behavior.

2 A collection of our motivations, needs, and preferences that—once understood—provides a blueprint to our strengths and weaknesses.

Synonyms: disposition, individuality

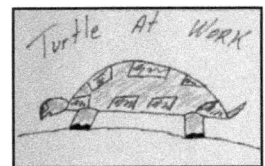

Continual Reflection & Learning

Begin this lesson by reading the quote in the sidebar and reflecting on this wisdom.

Successful leaders make time to reflect.

All successful leaders carve out time with their teams to think and dream collaboratively. Most have an additional practice of individual solitude.

Wouldn't it be ideal to be able to schedule brilliance or to brainstorm and find that inspiration on cue? Unfortunately, usually the best ideas come unpredictably amidst a wide-open space of time.

As you make a discipline of allowing space for reflection, you will begin to see the fruit of that practice.

But how? How can busy people find time to think?

Schedule it. Make an appointment with yourself and keep it. Don't allow others to book into that time. Don't allow yourself to reschedule.

Here are a few rhythms that allow for reflection:

DIVERT DAILY: Take the first five minutes of each day to think through the day ahead and engage in some disciplines to get your day off to the right start. At the end of each day, look back over what you have accomplished that day and prepare for the next day.

You can find team member Laurie Sorensen's Jumpstart and Power Down routines in the appendix. Here is a summary of how she diverts at the start and end of each workday:

- At the start of her day, she activates her core values by expressing gratitude and reading her personal mission and personal legacy statement. She also spends time in prayer to prepare her heart for the day. She then examines her schedule, noting her three priorities (Big Rocks) for the day.

- At the end of the day, she looks back over the day with gratitude and then looks ahead to the following day so she can anticipate and prepare for her most important initiatives. She 'brain dumps' any learnings that are in process or questions that she is pondering so that she can go home and fully transition from work.

WITHDRAW WEEKLY: One morning a week take two hours to focus. Look at the week ahead. Schedule your priorities so you are building in time to work on the goals you have said are important.

You have outlined how you will walk toward your personal and business legacy this week. Block time on your calendar to devote to each goal. Goals are not accomplished by accident. They take intentional focus.

Spend time thinking about something that's important and not urgent. This is a great time to work on a strategic project or to do some reflection.

QUIT QUARTERLY: Each quarter take a half-day and get out your Four Plans. During this time reflect on progress toward goals, update your plans with new goals, status updates, and clarify your priorities for the next quarter.

ABANDON ANNUALLY: Take a day to get away and plan. To reflect on the past year. To renew your legacy, life, and leadership plans for the next year. To just think. To spend time in quiet and solitude. To replenish.

This isn't the time to renew your business plan. Don't make the mistake of doing that plan alone. Instead, use this time to prepare to meet with your team and walk through the business plan or a strategic planning system.

A Lifestyle of Learning

You will never grow your company unless you grow your own abilities to lead and build the people who will build the business. The best leaders are those who are constantly learning and putting what they learn into action. They may not make huge leaps in their growth, but they repeatedly learn a little bit and implement what they learn. Over time, these consistent efforts add up to large-scale improvement.

Check the box next to the phrase that most closely describes your current attitude toward learning.

> ❏ **I learn something new daily and put it into practice.**

> ❏ **I go to all kinds of conferences but never implement what I learn.**

> ❏ **Who has time for learning? I am running my business.**

> ❏ **I was glad to get out of school so I didn't have to learn anymore.**

In a study of 6500 top executives, the difference between the A-Players and the C-Players was that the A-Players were continuous learners, reading on average 24 books a year (a mix of fiction and non-fiction) (Harnish, 2006).

How many books do you normally read in a year?

> ❏ **1-10**   ❏ **10-15**   ❏ **15-20**   ❏ **20+**

APPLICATION: How will you cultivate a discipline of reflection and a lifestyle of learning?

Which of the following ways successful leaders display an insatiable appetite to learn also describe you?	Current Habit	Habit to Form	Not Planning to Do
They are always reading or writing something.			
They are curious and ask lots of questions.			
They are often experimenting with new ways of doing something.			
They are reflective and frequently pause to analyze their own leadership behaviors and interpersonal interactions.			
They are humble and assume they don't know everything.			
They are willing to be vulnerable and admit their mistakes.			
They believe everyone has something to teach them.			
They embrace feedback and look for the grain of truth in every criticism.			

Live Your Plans

Begin this lesson by reading the quote in the sidebar and reflecting on this wisdom about the importance of executing.

In this lesson, we will examine perhaps THE singular most important step in being able to come to next year's planning session and celebrate a successful year. If you do this, you will see that you have made substantial progress both in your personal life and in business. It will be quickly apparent that you have led well and have made an impact that if repeated over the course of your lifetime and your tenure with your company, will lead to your desired legacy. What is that step? Breathing life into your plans. Action. Execution.

What would you list as some of the most common barriers to execution?

_____

According to an international survey of more than 13,000 people, the following are among the top barriers to execution:

- Lack of employee clarity of the objectives they were supposed to execute

- Lack of commitment to achieving the goal

- Lack of accountability for progressing on the goals

- Lack of collaborative team work

However, those barriers were not the most serious reason why people were not accomplishing their goals. The researchers discovered a fundamental problem with execution: your day job! (McChesney & Covey, 2012)

Many leaders spend their entire day just trying to put out fires and deal with operational issues that arise. Their constant reactive mindset makes it next to impossible to execute anything new because they are just trying to keep things afloat. They are in a cycle of being enslaved to the 'tyranny of the urgent' rather than stepping back and making sure they are executing on the important.

If you have made it this far in the book, you most likely are not among that crowd. You have seen the necessity of stepping back and taking time to plan. You are a strategic leader or are becoming a leader who thinks proactively.

So, how do you remove the barriers to execute effectively?

Reflect on what you value. If you say relationships are a priority for you, but you act like your tasks are the priority, your values and actions are misaligned. Keeping your core values central to your thinking will do more to help you live out your plans than anything else. Post them. Read them daily. Write about them and their connection to your goals. It may be the most powerful two minutes of your day.

> *It had long since come to my attention that people of accomplishment rarely sat back and let things happen to them. They went out and happened to things.*
> – Leonardo da Vinci

Stay focused. You will always have more ideas than you and/or your team can possibly execute. Use your plans as a filter. Say no to good ideas so that you can remain focused on your legacy vision.

It is a paradoxical principle but a true one nonetheless. When you find yourself getting mired in the 'daily,' step back and review your strategic objectives. Ask yourself, "Which strategic initiative am I uniquely equipped to help move forward for our company? What is my HABU (Highest and Best Use)?" Then do that.

Help your teammates to eat right (and eat right yourself). Often, we don't execute because the enormity of the goal scares us out of even beginning. You can help coach your team past their fears by teaching them how to break down a goal into manageable tasks.

Ask them simple guiding questions like, "What one thing would you do first? What would your next step be?" Then send them off to do those things. We eat an elephant one bite at a time. Help your team to take only bite-sized pieces and understand how to persistently persevere until the task is accomplished.

Ensure clarity. Communicate, re-communicate, and be sure to over-communicate the goals and objectives. This ensures each person knows the goal and what to do to achieve it.

Provide regular feedback. Have a feedback loop that provides you and your teammates with the ability to measure progress. Keep the numbers you are working toward visible and regularly update where you are in relation to the goal.

Celebrate accomplishment. When you reach a goal, take time to celebrate! Frame your mindset intentionally: The journey is about progress, not perfection. Small wins are indeed wins. One degree of change is still change. Give yourself grace and determinedly, doggedly commit to keep walking forward. Is an area of your life or business better today than it was yesterday? If so, press on.

Repeat the Process. You will find that if you repeatedly do the right things in the right way, you will achieve your goals. Small habits add up to a powerful track record of consistency.

Your legacy vision is uniquely glorious. Keep it in front of you and let it motivate you to action. It is faithfulness across the journey and choosing to take each next step that finally brings us to a successful finish.

One day you will look back and find that you have lived according to your priorities and accomplished what is truly important instead of just marching to the incessant drumbeat of the urgent.

Live and lead intentionally. Breathe life into your legacy vision, as you take one step at a time. The world is waiting. Go ignite success.

A Note From Our Team

Thank you for taking time to complete the very important process of planning your life and your business. You are now in a very special group of people, as very few will make the investment and spend the time doing the hard work it takes to plan. There is nothing miraculous about this way of planning. It is merely a simple framework to help get you started on the journey of creating a plan for how you live and lead. But it is a good starting point, and from here, you can launch into a lifetime of living according to plan.

The reality is that your planning is not complete; you have only just begun. Once you create your initial plans, it is time to review and update them. That is what makes planning so powerful. You write a plan, and then you regularly take time to review your progress. There are always items on the plan that have changed. That doesn't mean you failed in your planning; it means that life or business has changed and you need to revise the plan. These plans are living documents. They are not 'write once and file' at all. But each time you update, you are not starting from scratch but instead merely tweaking the plan to make it fit the reality of your circumstances at that time.

The templates are not sacred either. They are merely a place to begin. Over time, we would expect you will expand your plan significantly and move well past these templates. But we've learned that the hardest part of planning is getting started, so there is enough guidance in the templates to help you get something in place, and from that point, you can 'make it your own' and write the plans any way you see valuable. The impact of planning is not the document but the result that occurs when you execute against it.

That is the challenge that now lies ahead. Merely writing a plan, while a very good step, has little to no value if you don't do something. The first step should be to share it with those in your patch that it impacts. Start with your spouse and family—they will be impacted by the outcome of your plans most of all. But share it much more broadly. In your peer group, because they cannot hold you accountable if they are unaware of what you are trying to accomplish. Share it with people in your circle of friends – fellow church attendees, your neighbors you are close with, anyone who can help keep you on course. We recommend sharing with those on your inner team—attorney, CPA, banker, mentor—those you lean on for counsel and guidance. They need to have these plans as boundaries for the way you intend to live and lead.

Then it comes down to you. The rubber meets the road when you execute your plans. Until that point, this is a rather academic exercise. But we have had the privilege, first in our own lives and then in the lives of hundreds of other folks, to watch the power of planning change lives and businesses. We have been part of over one hundred peer group meetings. The most impactful meetings, without a shadow of a doubt, have been those revolving around planning. In particular, the meetings around legacy or life planning typically are the ones that are most memorable. Innumerable breakthroughs have occurred in relationships and personal growth when a leader shared their legacy or life plan with the group. It is amplified when their spouse has been in the room. Planning, but more accurately sharing those plans, is life changing.

Entrepreneur Arlin Sorensen shares, "For far too many years, I lived without really taking the time to plan. I met life as it happened to me, and because of my personality and upbringing, it seemed to work out pretty well. But the reality is that without a plan, we tend to drift a bit from our desired outcome.

That is most obvious in the area of life, where we typically are doing our own thing with little oversight or outside influence. We can quickly get into the weeds and then drive right into the ditch because we are living on the fly without having thought about the desired outcome we would like to achieve."

Planning doesn't prevent that from happening in and of itself. But planning along with accountability that drives the right execution can go a long way toward keeping you on the right path.

That is our desire for you—that you achieve your goals and dreams for your legacy, life, leadership, and business. The plans themselves won't accomplish that, but they provide a framework and guidance for those in your patch to use as you are kept accountable to your own plans. No one really likes accountability. But remember, you are providing the direction for what you want to be accountable to. These are your plans with your desired outcomes. All your accountability partners do is help keep you focused and on course. That is what will change your life and leadership. Don't stop with completing the plans. That is only the beginning. Share them broadly; ask some people to hold you accountable; then report transparently; receive their feedback with gratitude; make adjustments and keep marching toward your goals. It is exciting to think about what can happen with a little investment in writing plans and then living those out.

It is inevitable that everyone faces the end of life. In that moment, no one says, "I wish I had worked more hours and spent more time at the office." Yet many people lay on their deathbed saying through tears how they wished they had spent more time with their spouse, kids, parents, or other loved ones. There are no do-overs in life. We only get one chance to live it well.

These plans don't guarantee they will occur, but they do give you a framework and a methodology to use in effectively managing the most precious commodity we have — our 168 hours of time each week. Our success in living and leading depends heavily on how we use our time. Use these plans to help you determine where you invest that time. This is your matrix of saying yes or no to the hundreds of options you will face each week that want a piece of your time. You can be successful in doing that with some personal discipline and focus.

Thanks again for investing the time and effort into planning your life and leadership. It will serve you well. Feel free to reach out if you have questions or suggestions to make this workbook better. We want to empower people with the tools they need to gain control of their time and achieve the things they desire. Planning is one key part of that process. But it is a journey, not an event, and you need to keep working to refine and make it relevant to the circumstances of life as it faces you each day.

Blessings!

Your Hundredfold Harvest Team

Works Cited

Accountable. (2012). Retrieved October 19, 2012, from Dictionary.com: http://dictionary.reference. com/browse/ accountable

Build a Culture of Accountability. (2012). Retrieved October 19, 2012, from Driving Results through Culture: http://drivingresultsthroughculture.com/?p=3403

Core. (2012). Retrieved September 27, 2012, from Dictionary.com: http://dictionary.reference.com/ browse/core

Domain. (2017). As defined by the Paterson Center.

Execute. (2012). Retrieved October 8, 2012, from Dictionary.com: http://dictionary.reference.com/ browse/execute

Integrity. (2012). Retrieved September 26, 2012, from Dictionary.com: http://dictionary.reference.com/ browse/ integrity

Leadership. (2012). Retrieved October 8, 2012, from Dictionary.com: http://dictionary.reference.com/ browse/ leadership

Legacy. (2012). Retrieved October 4, 2012, from Dictionary.com: http://dictionary.reference.com/ browse/ legacy

Meeting. (2012). Retrieved October 23, 2012, from Dictionary.com: http://dictionary.reference.com/ browse/ meeting

Plan. (2012). Retrieved September 26, 2012, from Dictionary.com: http://dictionary.reference.com/ browse/plan

Planning. (2012, September 14). Retrieved September 26, 2012, from Wikipedia: http://en.wikipedia. org/wiki/ Planning

Priority. (2012). Retrieved October 5, 2012, from Dictionary.com: http://dictionary.reference.com/ browse/ priority

Strategy. (2012). Retrieved October 12, 2012, from Dictionary.com: http://dictionary.reference.com/ browse/ strategy

Time. (2012). Retrieved October 23, 2012, from Dictionary.com: http://dictionary.reference.com/ browse/time

Values. (2012). Retrieved September 27, 2012, from Dictionary.com: http://dictionary.reference.com/ browse/ value

Vision. (2012). Retrieved October 3, 2012, from Dictionary.com: http://dictionary.reference.com/ browse/vision

Bradberry, T. (2007). *Self-Awareness: The Hidden Driver of Success and Satisfaction.* New York: G.P. Putnam's Sons.

Collins, J. (2001). *Vision Framework.* Retrieved October 8, 2012, from Jim Collins.com: http://www. jimcollins. com/tools/vision-framework.pdf

EMyth Synotac. (2012). *State of the Business Owner.*

Harnish, V. (2006). *Mastering the Rockefeller Habits.* New York: SelectBooks.

Little, D. L. (2011). *Make a Difference: The Challenge of Excellence.* Decatur: The Enrichment Center.

McChesney, C., & Covey, S. (2012). *The 4 Disciplines of Execution.* New York: Free Press.

NTL Institute for Applied Behavioral Science. (n.d.). *The Learning Pyramid.* Alexandria, VA.

Stanley, A. (2008). *The Principle of the Path*, pg 14. Nashville: Thomas Nelson, Inc.

[1]Harter, J., & Mann, A. (2017, April 12). The Right Culture: Not Just About Employee Satisfaction. Retrieved from https://www.gallup.com/workplace/236366/right-culture-not-employee-satisfaction. aspx

Appendix

List of Values

Abundance	Commitment	Eagerness
Acceptance	Communication	Education
Accountability	Community	Effectiveness
Accomplishment	Compassion	Efficiency
Accuracy	Competence	Elation
Achievement	Competition	Elegance
Acknowledgement	Concentration	Empathy
Adaptability	Confidence	Encouragement
Adventure	Connection	Endurance
Affection	Consciousness	Energy
Aggressiveness	Consistency	Enjoyment
Agility	Contentment	Enthusiasm
Alertness	Content over fluff	Equality
Ambition	Continuity	Excellence
Anticipation	Continuous	Excitement
Appreciation	Improvement	Experience
Assertiveness	Contribution	Expertise
Attentiveness	Control	Exploration
Audacity	Conviction	Expressiveness
Awareness	Convincing	Fairness
Balance	Cooperation	Faith
Beauty	Courage	Fame
Belonging	Courtesy	Family
Blissfulness	Creativity	Fidelity
Boldness	Curiosity	Flexibility
Bravery	Daring	Flow
Brilliance	Decisiveness	Focus
Calm	Delight	Forgiveness
Candor	Dependability	Fortitude
Carefulness	Desire	Freedom
Caring	Determination	Friendship
Certainty	Devotion	Frugality
Challenge	Dignity	Fun
Change	Diligence	Generosity
Charity	Discipline	Giving
Cheerfulness	Discovery	Going the Extra Mile
Clarity	Discretion	Goodness
Cleanliness	Diversity	Grace
Collaboration	Drive	Gratitude
Comfort	Duty	Growth

Guidance	Love	Quality
Happiness	Making a Difference	Quiet
Harmony	Mastery	Rationality
Hard work	Maturity	Recognition
Health	Meaning	Relationships
Helpfulness	Merit	Reliability
Heroism	Mindfulness	Religion
Holiness	Modesty	Resourcefulness
Honesty	Money	Respect
Honor	Motivation	Responsibility
Hopefulness	Nonviolence	Righteousness
Hospitality	Openness	Risk-Taking
Humility	Opportunity	Romance
Humor	Optimism	Safety
Imagination	Order	Security
Independence	Organization	Selflessness
Influence	Originality	Self-esteem
Ingenuity	Outcome	Seriousness
Inner Peace	Orientation	Service
Innovation	Outstanding Service	Simplicity
Insightfulness	Passion	Sincerity
Inspiration	Peace	Skill
Integrity	Perceptiveness	Speed
Intelligence	Perseverance	Spirit
Intensity	Persistence	Stability
Intimacy	Personal growth	Strength
Intuitiveness	Pleasure	Style
Inventiveness	Poise	Systemization
Investing	Positive attitude	Teamwork
Joy	Power	Timeliness
Justice	Practicality	Tolerance
Kindness	Precision	Tradition
Knowledge	Preparedness	Tranquility
Leadership	Presence	Trust
Learning	Preservation	Truth
Liberty	Privacy	Unity
Logic	Proactivity	Variety
Longevity	Progress	Well-Being
Love	Prosperity	Wisdom
Loyalty	Punctuality	

RESPECT

Unbiased consideration and regard for the rights, values, beliefs, and property of all people

HONESTY

Straightforwardness, sincerity, truthfulness

HUMILITY

Having a modest opinion or estimate of one's own importance, rank, etc.

INTEGRITY

Consistency in character and behavior; no matter one's location or present company; 'walking your talk.'

FAIRNESS

Treating people equally; acting free of bias or injustice; evenhandedness

HEALTH

Physical and mental well-being

BALANCE

Intentionally allocating time and energy between one's professional and personal life (recognizing this will vary based on a season of life)

FAITH

Living the reality that everything happens for a reason

COMPETITION
Having a strong desire to compete and win or to succeed.

COMPASSION
Understanding the suffering of others and wanting to do something about it

FREEDOM
The power to act, speak, or think without externally imposed restraints

DEDICATION
The act of binding yourself (intellectually or emotionally) to a course of action; commitment

FAMILY
Spending both quality and quantity time with those about whom one cares most

ACCOUNTABILITY
Being obliged to answer for one's own actions and the outcomes of those actions

GIVING/SERVICE
Making monetary and time donations to benefit others

TEAMWORK
Collaborating by fulfilling a role within a group to achieve a goal

HUMOR

The ability to laugh at oneself and find humor in all things

CONSISTENCY

Steadfast adherence to the same principles, course, form, etc.; a pattern of behavior or action.

TRUSTWORTHINESS

Dependability, deserving of confidence

COURAGE

Quality of mind or spirit that enables one to face difficulty, danger, paint, etc., without fear; bravery

LOYALTY

Faithfulness to another person or group

WEALTH

Desire for substantial monetary income

SECURITY

Having the essentials one needs to live and be safe

RECOGNITION

To receive special attention, to feel important

EXCELLENCE

The pursuit of mastery and achievement of quality; professionalism

STRUCTURE

Established processes and systems

MORALITY

Desire for high ethical standards; a strong sense of right and wrong

PATIENCE

The capacity for enduring hardship or inconvenience

CONSENSUS

Agreement; accord; harmony; general agreement

SUCCESS

Attainment of professional position, favor, or eminence; achieving your goals

RESPONSIBILITY

Reliability or dependability

POWER

Ability to lead, direct, persuade, control

HELPFULNESS
Sense of concern for and outreach to the needs of others

CURIOSITY
Seeking and learning new information and insights

WISDOM
The ability to apply knowledge, experience, understanding, common sense, and insight

INDEPENDENCE
Freedom from control or influence of another or others, self sufficient

GROWTH
Investing in habits of personal and professional learning and development

LEGACY
Focus on the impact of a life well lived and a business well run

KNOWLEDGE
The pursuit of intellectual endeavors and the gaining of understanding; education

INTIMACY
Close and deep relationships

LEADERSHIP
The ability to motivate others towards the achievement of a goal

COMMUNITY
Cooperation with others with shared interests

CREATIVITY
Imagination, inspiration, and inventiveness; innovation

ADVENTURE
Participation in activities that involve excitement and risk

HAPPINESS/JOY
Feelings of contentment, satisfaction, and fulfillment

FRIENDSHIP
Comradeship; good-fellowship

FUN
Play, laughter, and the ability to be amused

OPTIMISM
Tendency to look on the more favorable side of events or conditions and expect the most favorable outcome

Core Values Tool

Your values are your navigation system for life. Getting them defined and properly calibrated is one of the most important steps in directing your life toward your grandest vision.

The below series of questions are designed to help you evaluate and refine what is truly important to you and what matters most in life. Perhaps not every question will be helpful for you; but I encourage you to read through them thoughtfully, and allow the questions to provoke thought as you select the top half-dozen values for your life.

1. Who is the person I respect most in life?

_____

_____

2. What are their core values?

_____

_____

3. Who is my best friend, and what are his/her top three qualities?

_____

_____

4. If I could have more of any one quality instantly, what would it be?

_____

_____

5. What are three qualities in people that make me angry when I encounter them?

_____

_____

6. Which personality trait, attribute, or quality do people compliment me on the most?

_____

_____

7. What are the three most important values I want to pass on to my children?

_____

_____

8. If I were to teach a graduating high-school class values that would give them the best opportunity for success in life, what would those be and why?

_____

_____

9. If I had enough money to retire tomorrow, which values would I continue to hold?

_____

_____

10. Which values do I see being valid 100 years from now?

_____

_____

11. The top dozen qualities of the 'ideal' man or woman

_____

_____

Top Ten Values

Now take a look at your answers above. Do you notice any reoccurring themes? Taking what you've observed in others, what others have observed about you, what you want for others, and things you would fight for or against, create a list of your top 10 values (in any order) below.

#	CORE VALUE
1	
2	
3	
4	
5	
6	
7	
8	
9	
10	

Now, let's reduce it down to the half-dozen most important to you. Put a star by the values you're sure about. Then take the ones you feel are important but aren't sure if they're top-six material and put them in pairs.

Think about two of those values side-by-side, and ask yourself which of the two is more important, eliminating the other.

Keep pitting the survivors against each other until you're down to six. If some of the values you listed are just two words describing the same idea, combine them.

Top Six Values:

Now prioritize your core values in order of importance, with the most important first. All are important, of course, but which are the most important? If you had to choose between two values, which would you fight for, or even die defending?

Feel free to have less values than six. Six is not a magic number. So list at least three values but no more than six.

MY TOP SIX VALUES IN LIFE IN PRIORITY ORDER ARE:

#	CORE VALUE
1	
2	
3	
4	
5	
6	

Values Definition Template

Now write a definition of each. What does each value look like when lived out the way you believe it should be in your life?

EXAMPLE:

Value: Integrity	
Definition	Doing the right thing, no matter who (if anyone) is watching.
Behaviors	Tell the truth at all times Treat all people with equal value Be ethical in all things

Below, there are blank charts for your use.

CORE VALUE 1:	
Definition	
Behaviors	

CORE VALUE 2:	
Definition	
Behaviors	

CORE VALUE 3:	
Definition	
Behaviors	

CORE VALUE 4:	
Definition	
Behaviors	

CORE VALUE 5:	
Definition	
Behaviors	

CORE VALUE 6:	
Definition	
Behaviors	

ACCi

ACCi was founded in late 1989 out of the belief that businesses needed a professional advisor (much like CPAs & Attorneys) to help them understand how to best implement and use technology, as opposed to a computer company that just sold them computer equipment.

In March of 1990, Bobby Welch joined the startup to build a software development division and to provide managerial oversight. In April 1997, Keith Keller (life-long friend and college roommate) moved back to Birmingham and joined ACCi to build a formal sales & marketing division. In 2001, the partners bought out the founder and have been building the business since.

ACCi is passionate about their culture because they view it as the axis on which their business spins. Bobby shares, "We will not be successful if our team does not feel engaged, valued, and a part of our overall story. That is why it so critical that we consistently communicate and the team has clarity around our 'why,' 'what,' and 'how we behave.'"

Culture is what the ACCi leadership looks for first when hiring, then for experience/skills as they measure the aptitude and desire each candidate possesses to learn and grow the ACCi way.

The culture at ACCi is based around faith (honoring a higher power through their business), family (providing well for their families), and service (serving clients with excellence by building strong relationships).

ACCi has kindly provided some of the elements that make up their principled culture:

- Beliefs and Attitudes (A Culture Guide for the ACCi team)

- Who We Are (Customer-Facing Communication of Culture)

- Our Mission

- Our Core Values

Beliefs and Attitudes

Our Team Only Recruits 'A' Players
Why surround yourself with mediocrity when you can be part of an exceptional team? We don't have room for 'C' players on this team. 'B' players should be constantly striving to become 'A' players.

Let's Not Reach the Bar, Let's Stand On the Bar
It's always good to know what the minimum levels are. But let's not settle for the minimum; instead, let's exceed the minimum bar, and exceed other's expectations.

We like to work as a team
We work together—literally in the same room—and enjoy the camaraderie that we find in that environment. Show up at the office, enjoy the fellowship, the learning, the sharing of best practices. If you want to be a lone wolf, ours is not the team for you.

No One Person is Greater
Never ask someone to do something you aren't willing to do yourself. If you think it's beneath you, then you probably need to get off that high stool and stand together with the rest of us.

Humor Helps
Some people believe that yelling helps—it doesn't. Sometimes you just have to laugh at what life serves you. Everyone appreciates a smile over a frown.

Process is Good
Remember that project we did last year that went well—what did we learn from it, and how do we repeat it? Remember that project that didn't go so well—how do we avoid that again? Processes and systems establish a baseline, and enable us to effectively improve as we deliver our services. Systems and processes allow us to avoid headaches as we grow.

Full Disclosure
Doctors help patients make informed decisions by being honest about their condition. IT companies help businesses make wise decisions about technology by being honest about the condition of their infrastructure. No one likes a surprise when it could have been avoided by being up front with the facts.

Document, Document, Document
Ever wonder why other people don't think like you think? Because they are not you. So when you find yourself thinking 'it's so obvious,' think again. Document your thoughts, your data gathering, your processes, etc. then share it with others, and you will soon find that others are thinking like you think.

Rocket Ships, Race Cars, Lightning Bolts
Yep, we said it. That's the stuff we are made of. And we enjoy it. Researching technology and its applications to our customers is necessary, takes time, and can even be fun. So be proud that you like rocket ships and lightning bolts, because that translates to helping clients.

Who We Are

ACCi is not just a technology company. We are a relationship building company that uses technology to promote the success of our clients.

People serving people—that's the way we see it.

Our 'Why'
To improve the lives of our clients and employees through proven, innovative technologies. That's it.

Improving the lives of our clients manifests itself in many ways—systems they don't have to worry about, improved operational efficiency, a better bottom-line, and more time away from work with the family. If the technologies we provide and manage help to achieve these things in the lives of our clients, then we have fulfilled our 'Why.'

IT Is an Investment
Not an expense. We want to work with businesses that view their information technology as a competitive advantage and see the value of investing in their people, keeping their IT current, maintaining it effectively, and improving the operational maturity level of their organization.

Our People
It's our team that makes the difference. What sets our group apart is the unique combination of skill sets, longevity, attitude, and teamwork. We own the problem, from the beginning of the response or project, until the end. Our people have that 'stick-to-it-ness' that makes them so valuable to our clients—clients that ask for technical staff by name. Like the Navy Seals, our team is comprised of a unique blend of talents, tools, intuitiveness, and insight—a blend that gets results, every time.

We Want to Give Back
Involvement in the community is a part of being a responsible business citizen in the areas in which we operate. We can't make the world a better place unless we are willing to give of our time, our resources, and our finances.

ACCi's long-term goal is to leave our fingerprints on the lives of those around us in the hopes that we all find our lives enriched as a family. To that end, some of the ways in which ACCi is involved and gives back to our community include the following:

- Camp NorthStar Inner City Summer Camp
- M-Power Ministries Sing & Shout
- SafeHouse of Shelby County
- Restoration Academy
- The Bell Center

- Boy Scouts & Basketball
- Sponsor Youth Baseball & Basketball Teams
- City Salesmans Club
- Kiwanis Club of Homewood-Mountain Brook

Our Mission

To serve our clients as the recognized leader in providing professional services and proven technology solutions for business, while maintaining honest profits and a team spirit that encourages growth and development.

Our Core Values

Clients

The complete satisfaction of our clients is our top priority, which produces enduring relationships built on confidence and trust in ACCi's ability and desire to provide superior service and solutions to meet their technology needs.

Integrity

Uncompromised character, honesty, and a commitment to personal excellence provide the foundation on which all of our business dealings are based. Our mandate is to be technically competent, professional in presentation, and sincerely courteous in all we say and do.

Service

We will consistently provide valuable, responsive technical service and support that exceeds our clients' expectations. Our commitment to serving our clients should not only be evident to them, but also should govern our internal attitudes and dialogue regarding their unique needs.

Team

We must daily promote an environment that reflects our commitment to serving each other as members of a unified and interdependent team. Our mission will only be achieved when our internal attitude is one of cooperation, single mindedness, and trust.

Profit

We are committed to meeting our profit objectives in order to sustain the growth of the company, to fairly compensate our employees, and to offer products and services of the highest quality.

bmcnetworks inc.
TECHNOLOGY SERVICES

BMC Networks is a 25-person managed service provider (MSP) located in the downtown core of Vancouver, BC, Canada. It is an example of an MSP that focuses on serving a single vertical and has a culture reflective of the vertical they serve.

BMC was started in 1997, when founder Brian Mauch graduated from the University of British Columbia with degrees in Commerce and Law, and combined his education with his passion for technology to start his own business providing IT services for law firms.

BMC Networks has graciously provided a vignette about the elements of their workplace culture that have created an environment of professionals serving other professionals:

- Core Values

- Diverse Workforce

- Team Building

- Unique Benefits

- Recognition

BMC Networks began with a verticalized focus on the legacy industry and still specializes in law firms, which comprise 95% of the clientele. Since BMC's client base consists of professionals, all BMC employees dress and conduct themselves professionally, and work in a professional office setting.

BMC's core values are:

- **Integrity:** We do what we say we will do.

- **Service:** We exist to serve our clients and each other.

- **Professionalism:** We are the professional IT company for professional service firms.

- **Unity:** We are all equally responsible for our success.

- **Fun:** We take our work seriously, but not ourselves.

BMC has a diverse workforce that takes pride in working at such a progressive employer. Women are represented in the administrative, technical, and management teams, and compose 30% of the company's workforce, which is higher than the average MSP. BMC is also culturally diverse, with half of the team members being born outside of North America. This creates an interesting, dynamic environment where learning and communication is key. BMC is also a LGBTQ-friendly space, ensuring everyone is given a safe and rewarding experience at the workplace.

BMC is known for the annual parties, all paid for by the company. The annual Christmas party is celebrated with employees and their significant others at a fine dining restaurant, with either a night at a nearby hotel or safe passage home provided for employees. The summer BBQ includes employees' families, and is catered at a heritage restaurant with a lakeside lawn setting.

Regular team-building events are provided after work throughout the year, occurring approximately every two months. Team-building events have included archery tag, a team scavenger hunt, escape rooms, laser tag, sword-fighting training, pitch-and-putt, and go-karting. We also offer a dinner out with the after-work team-building events.

At the office, coffee, pop, and juice are supplied for employees in the kitchen. Fruit and other healthy snacks are also provided. Every Friday, a catered lunch is presented to all staff, called 'the weekly all-hands meeting.' This usually includes a lunch-and-learn event presented by a team member, with no restrictions on who can participate. Every Friday at 4:00pm, work is halted and the 'Brew-haha' happy hour begins: drinks, food, video games, and occasionally (to the chagrin of our office neighbours) karaoke are enjoyed by all employees.

In addition to covering 100% of extended health premiums (including vision and dental), BMC provides two unique annual benefits:

1. Every employee gets to select their own birthday gift from BMC, to a maximum value of $500, as a non-taxable benefit. It is intended to be for something special that they can spoil themselves with, and the type of gifts selected have been as diverse as our employees.

2. We also want to encourage health and wellness, and to that end we provide an annual reimbursement of items or services related to health and wellness, to a maximum of $500. Frequent selections include gym memberships and sports equipment.

BMC is the home of the 'IT Ninjas.' Peers nominate a 'Ninja of the Month,' and winners are awarded ninja figurines to proudly display on their desks, and an annual 'Samurai of the Year' winner is awarded a framed samurai print which hangs on our walls. Employees who have served five years at BMC get to choose a replica ninja sword which will hang on the wall of fame.

BMC is a family for the employees that work here. Exciting news is celebrated, support is offered to those who need it, and long lasting friendships form; enduring even when one member returns to New Zealand, or another decides to stay at home with his new baby. Ties like these are created through an atmosphere of trust and openness, and BMC works hard at maintaining that culture.

Charles IT

Charles IT, owned by HTG member Foster Charles, is a company founded by millennials that prides itself on being a place where people love to work.

As a child, Foster could be found taking apart anything electronic—from a remote control to an entire television. He just had to know how everything worked. As he grew older, his friends and family relied on him for help fixing their computers and electronics, and so in 2006, Charles IT was born.

Foster's commitment to building a strong culture is evident not only to his team but is also known within the community. He has been invited several times to share about the unique aspects of the company culture and how to attract and keep good employees.

Charles IT has graciously shared some of the elements that make up their winsome culture that they use to attract strong team members:

- Our Philosophy (Core Values)

- Top 10 Reasons to Work for Charles IT

- Employee Benefits

- Join the Force! How We Market Our Culture to Potential Team Members

Core Values

Exceptional Service

While we're a technology company, we also happen to have ridiculously good customer service skills! We understand that your business is your top priority, so we make it our priority to help you succeed. Consider us your personal IT concierge.

Passionate People

Our team of exceptional people is what makes our company stand out. Everyone is encouraged to grow and succeed, which reflects in the exceptional support and service we provide to our customers.

Constant Communication

We understand communication is key, so we keep you in the loop at all times. We also give you full access to monitor our progress. (Feel free to stalk us while we work!)

Honest and Forthright

We keep our promises, fulfill our commitments, and follow though. We demand your feedback (yes, sometimes with pesky surveys!), so we can keep improving.

Endless Improvement

We believe in implementing cutting edge technology and we love our 'shiny toys.' Plus we constantly upgrade our services and policies and keep up with the latest IT developments and certifications.

Top 10 Reasons to Work for Charles IT

1. **You'll take pride in being a part of a 'small business'** – At Charles IT you're not just stuck in a cubicle. This company requires you to collaborate and communicate with all coworkers and clients. You'll get to enjoy meeting new people and taking part of the business.

2. **Handsome benefits** – At Charles IT, the traditional benefits of Medical, Dental, Life, Long Term Disability, Profit Sharing, and 401k are offered—along with some not so traditional benefits such as free dry cleaning, fun company-provided Friday Lunches, an automatic 3% contribution from the company to your 401k, and bonuses determined by your quarterly performance reviews. Even more exciting, enjoy a fully stocked kitchen on hand for when hunger strikes as well as exciting quarterly team-building outings.

3. **Experience a positive and fun corporate culture** – Everyone at Charles IT is passionate about their work. We take pride in our services and enjoy technology because it ignites a fire inside of us. So when seeking new members, we want the best of the best—people who share in our passion.

4. **Enjoy stability, consistency, and integrity in leadership** – Foster Charles founded the company when he was 17-years old and displays unwavering commitment to the company and its employees. Decisions are always made based on what is best for everyone and the company's future. Foster has eliminated the hierarchical structure of business and works on the front lines with all other employees. Foster is always present and willing to help employees in or out of the office. The company prides itself on maintaining stability with a minimum of a six-month cushion of operating income, leaving the remainder of profit to be allocated for bonuses, charitable donations, an office wish-list of new technology, and other expenses.

5. **Excitement in working for a company that continues to grow** – Charles IT consistently refuses more business than it accepts. The company is strategic in its vision for growth and is continuously expanding by selecting the right clients and the right vendors, at the right times.

6. **Recognition and appreciation for being a special part of the team** – Every three months progress is tracked and recognition is provided in ways beyond monetary compensation. Charles IT recognizes everyone's individual care and commitment to making the company successful.

7. **Cutting edge equipment** – Here at Charles IT, we like our toys. Often the office buys equipment and receives demos far in advance before they are even released to the general public. If you enjoy getting your hands on the latest technology, this is the place to be.

8. **Opportunities for professional development and individual growth** – Every Friday after lunch, the team participates in one hour of training to benefit the entire team as well as our clients. Also, employees may enjoy continued learning—

all training materials and your first shot at a test or certification is paid for by the company.

9. **Flexibility and 'breaking corporate' mentality** – There is no rigid corporate structure or protocol. Charles IT is a homegrown business with corporate sensibility. We offer compressed work weeks, commissions on new business brought in by employees, and flexible hours.

10. **Team building** – Frequent team-building meetings and outings take place. Enjoy going to dinner with colleagues or various other events such as zip lining, concerts and performances, ice skating in New York City, and more. Feel good about working hard and playing hard with like-minded co-workers and clients.

Benefits

- **Dry Cleaning:** Being and looking smart go hand in hand. Any clothing you use for work is paid for once a week!
- **401K:** We're all looking forward to retirement on the beach, so we invest 3% in your 401K with each paycheck, no match required!
- **Fully Stocked Kitchen:** Including your favorite snack or caffeinated beverage
- **Compressed Work Weeks:** Need a day off, but don't want to use your PTO? We work with you to make up the hours.
- **Medical:** With our action-packed company outings, and life's many surprises… we figured we should have some serious health care plans.
- **Dental:** Have a sweet tooth? Don't worry, we have the dental department 'filled.'
- **Vision:** Can you read this? We thought so…
- **Life Insurance:** Nobody wants to talk about it, but it's good to know we have you and your family covered.
- **Long-Term Disability:** So your family doesn't have to worry about our crazy outings.
- **Short-Term Disability:** Clumsy? Don't worry, we've got your back.
- **Quarterly Team Building:** Ever wish you could work at the beach, fly a helicopter into the Grand Canyon, or drive a Ferarri? Each quarter, we go on a surprise outing for fun.
- **Birthday Off:** Getting older is tough.
- **Friday Lunch:** Lunch is on us every Friday!
- **Paid Time Off:** Climbing Machu Pichu, Cruise to Fiji, Swimming with Polar Bears…PTO makes this possible.
- **Corporate Concierge:** We have an amazing office 'butler' who will change your car oil, take your dog for a pedicure, or pick up that anniversary gift you forgot to get…
- **Dogs:** Bring your fur-iend to work. Just make sure he wears his CIT office bandana!
- **Fitness Reimbursement:** You don't always go to the gym, but when you do, you get reimbursed for it.
- **Paid Certification Tests:** We like smart people. Any certification you pass is on us!
- **Training:** Need more EXP points? We provide you with any books, prep-exams, and courses you need to get the training you want.

**The Final
Final
Step.**

Professional IT

The Final Step

The Final Step is a London IT firm that specializes in serving professional services firms, building trusted partnerships with clients.

Managing Director Raja Pagadala founded The Final Step in 1987, based on two principles dear to his heart. Firstly, how to get technology working to people's advantage. Second, providing a service that inspires lifetime loyalty. He has built a culture that treats others as people first and employees or client companies second. His team builds direct, personal relationships with their customers.

After reading *The Advantage* by Patrick Lencioni, The Final Step management team created a one-page playbook which is an internal facing document. It provides clarity to the team around the important questions of who, what, why, and how The Final Step does business. It helps The Final Step to be a healthy and smart organization, both internally and externally.

The Final Step graciously shared their playbook which answers the following questions:

- Why do we exist? (Mission Statement/Core Purpose)

- How do we behave? (Core Values)

- What do we do?

- How will we succeed? (Differentiators)

- What is important right now? (Current priorities)

- Who does what? (Delineation of duties among management)

TFS Annual Playbook

Why do we exist?

We exist to enable people to fulfil their potential. By people, we mean colleagues, clients, suppliers, and the broader community.

> "Our core purpose is to create trust and value for our clients, to earn their lifetime loyalty and promotion."

How do we behave?

	We do:	We do not:
Respectful	Treat others as we would like to be treated.	Be rude, unprofessional, or belittle people.
Honest	Do the right thing.	Hide our mistakes.
Helpful	Share responsibilities and goals.	Consider things beneath us.

What do we do?

IT support and advice to help businesses succeed by fulfilling their potential.

How will we succeed?

Differentiate ourselves by providing effective, personalised service, promoting our culture, and leveraging smart thinking.

What is important right now?

This Year's Theme: Clients' Point of View (CPoV)
This Year's Key Phrase: Clarity of Communication

Management team: who does what currently?

Name	Title	Responsibility
Raja	Managing Director	Ensure long-term sustained success of TFS. Developing staff; client relationships; sales; finance.
Simon	Director	Marketing. Sales / account management; legals and health & safety.
Mansukh	Customer Service Manager	CSAT (Customer Satisfaction) Smiley faces and JYE reporting; internal QA.
Steve	Technical Manager	Projects / L3 technical team. All technical staff; technical standards, R&D, internal IT; account management.
Luisa	General Manager	All non-technical staff. Help RP in broad development of TFS.

Mytech Partners

Documentation Objective

The objective of this document is to define the new framework for the Culture Team at all Mytech sites. It is encouraged for this document to change with the ever-changing needs of the culture. Changes must be ratified between all site GM's and the CEO of Mytech.

Culture Team Mission

Maintain conditions suitable for growth

Communication Strategy

The Culture Team is only as good as its ability to communicate effectively with the rest of the organization. The following is a list of ways to ensure the Culture Team achieves that successful communication:

- **Regularly Scheduled Town Hall Meetings**
  - This will be the primary platform for all Mytech employees to get updates on active culture initiatives.
  - Town Hall meetings will give all Mytech employees an opportunity to voice any culture related ideas or concerns.
  - Town Hall meeting will be held at a minimum of quarterly.
- **Monthly Culture Newsletter**
  - This will be a global Mytech newsletter with input from each site.
- **Culture Board**
- **O365 Culture Video Channel**
- **Culture Updates at All Company Meetings**
- **Ambassadors of Each Site Will Meet at a Minimum Quarterly**
  - This provides an opportunity to share ideas of what is and isn't working.

Culture Team Design Strategy

There are two parts to the design of the Culture Team. The Core Culture Team and Cell Culture Teams. The Core Culture Team consists of the admin functionality for culture, which includes the Ambassador and Secretary roles. These team members have a minimum of a 14-month term. The Core Culture Team is responsible for moving forward key initiatives and recruiting for Cell Culture Teams. Led by a Core Team member, the Cell Culture Teams will focus on a very specific initiative until completion. Once the initiative is completed, the Cell Culture Team will disband. The design here is to embrace the old adage of many hands make light work. This provides opportunities for others to participate in culture with a smaller term commitment. At the same time allowing implementation of more cultural initiatives.

Culture Core Team Breakdown

The total number of members of the Culture Team will equal 10% of the site's staff. There is a minimum of three and a maximum of seven members per team.

- **Ambassador**
  - The general manager will identify a minimum of two individuals that they would feel confident in filling the position.
  - Majority vote during the annual Culture Team election will determine who will fill the position.
  - A Mytech BOD, coach, or manager cannot fill the ambassador position.
  - The term for this position is a minimum of a 14-month commitment.
- **Secretary**
  - This position will be voted on by the Culture Team members.
- **Members**
  - Any Mytech employee can fill a member's position.
  - The term for this position is a minimum of a 14-month commitment.

Culture Team Member's Responsibilities

- To ensure that the Culture Team's mission is lived out in accordance to the Mytech mission, vision, and values.
- Assisting in the advancement and maintenance of cultural initiatives.
- Actively recruit others within the organization to help facilitate cultural initiatives.
- Attend Culture Team and Town Hall meetings.
- Assist GM with annual culture awards.
- Members will hold each other accountable to the responsibilities stated in this framework document.
- Members are encouraged to embrace the values of Mytech to work out any points of contention on the team with final mediation by the GM if necessary.

Culture Team Secretary Responsibilities

- All above team member's responsibilities apply.
- Monitor and respond to the Culture Team email box.
- Monitor and report on submissions to the suggestion box.
- Capture minutes at Culture Team and Town Hall meetings or delegate to another member to capture minutes.
- Submit monthly material for the culture newsletter to the marketing team or delegate out.

Culture Team Ambassador Responsibilities

- All above team member's responsibilities apply.

MYTECH PARTNERS

- Meet a minimum of quarterly with the general manager to ensure that there is clarity of direction for the Culture Team and to report back on the cultural pulse of the organization.
- Facilitator of regularly scheduled Culture Team and Town Hall meetings unless delegated to another member.
- Report to the leadership team if the GM requests.
- Ensure that the Culture Team stays within the defined budget for the team and initiatives as defined by the general manager.
- Facilitate culture interviews.

Yearly Culture Team Election

- One week before the election, employees interested in volunteering for the Culture Team should email culture of their interest.
- Election is on the last full week of January and opened for one week.
- Terms are for 14-months with overlap of the last two months of the current team member and the first two months of the new team member. This is to ensure continuity of initiatives during team member transitions. Terms start on February 1 and end on March 31.
- The ballot will consist of all employees that have volunteered to be on the Culture Team and the minimum of two ambassador candidates chosen by the GM.
- Employees will vote for whom they would like to see on that team and the ambassador. The number of team members voted for will be based on the size of the team for that site.
- Culture Team membership is based on majority vote in the case of a tie the drawing of straws.

Culture Interviewing Questions

Communication:

1. What would you most like to learn here that would help you in the future?
2. How do you rely on others to make you better?
3. Tell me about the last time a co-worker or customer got angry with you. What happened?
4. Why do you want to work at this company and what are your expectations?
5. Tell me about a time you felt company leadership was wrong. What did you do?
6. Describe a time you felt you were right but you still had to follow directions or guidelines.
7. What do you think of your previous boss?
8. What are you most proud of?
9. What is your personal mission statement?
10. What are three positive things your last boss would say about you?

11. What negative thing would your last boss say about you?
12. What three character traits would your friends use to describe you?
13. If you were interviewing someone for this position, what traits would you look for?
14. List five words that describe your character.
15. Who has impacted you most in your career and how?
16. Tell me the difference between good and exceptional.
17. How do you think I rate as an interviewer?
18. When you work with a team, describe the role that you are most likely to play on the team.
19. Describe the color yellow to somebody who's blind.
20. Describe a situation you feel you should have handled differently.

Happiness:

1. What business would you love to start?
2. What's your superpower?
3. Who would win in a fight between Spiderman and Batman?
4. What are your lifelong dreams?
5. Tell me about your proudest achievement.
6. Who do you admire most and why?
7. What is your favorite memory from childhood?
8. What do you like to do for fun?
9. Who are your heroes?
10. What's your favorite 90's jam?
11. Who inspires you and why?
12. What movie, no matter how many times you've seen it, do you have to watch when it's on?
13. If you could be any character in fiction, whom would you be?
14. What's the best movie you've seen in the last year?
15. If you had only six months left to live, what would you do with the time?
16. If you could have dinner with anyone from history, who would it be and why?
17. If you won $20 million in the lottery, what would you do with the money?
18. If you were a car, what type would you be?

Accountability:

1. What is the toughest decision you had to make in the last few months?
2. What motivates you to come to work every day?
3. If someone wrote a biography about you, what do you think the title should be?
4. Who was your favorite manager and why?
5. What is your biggest regret and why?
6. Why did you choose you're major?
7. What are the qualities of a good leader? A bad leader?
8. Do you think a leader should be feared or liked?
9. How do you feel about taking no for an answer?
10. How would you feel about working for someone who knows less than you?
11. How would coworkers describe the role that you play on a team?
12. Provide an example of a time when you went out of your way and jumped through hoops to delight a customer.
13. Tell us about a decision that you made that was made based primarily on customer needs and input.
14. In the news story of your life, what would the headline say?
15. What is the most stressful situation you have handled and what was the outcome?
16. What were you doing the last time you looked at a clock and realized you had lost all track of time?
17. What will you miss about your present/last job?
18. What is your greatest achievement outside of work?

Improvement:

1. What book do you think everyone on the team should read?
2. If you woke up and had 2000 unread emails and could only answer 300 of them, how would you choose which ones to answer?
3. Was there a person in your career who really made a difference?
4. What do you ultimately want to become?
5. What are three positive character traits you don't have?
6. What's the most important thing you learned in school?
7. What's the last book you read?
8. If you had six months with no obligations or financial constraints, what would you do with the time?
9. What kind of personality do you work best with and why?
10. If you had to be shipwrecked on a deserted island, but all your human needs—such as food and water—were taken care of, what two items would you want to have with you?
11. There's no right or wrong answer, but if you could be anywhere in the world right now, where would you be?
12. What makes you want to learn?
13. How would you go about making Mytech better?
14. What do you bring to a company that you feel benefits them?
15. What are your goals?
16. Describe a situation in which you inspired trust and respect in your team.

17. What key factors drive you?
18. What attracts you to the current position you are applying for?
19. What are your career goals and where do you see yourself five years from now?

Culture Interview Training

- **What We Want Out of the Interview**
  - We want the interviewee's guard to be let down. They have already been vetted for their ability to do the job, now we want to get to know them: how they interact with themselves, with others, with a team, etc.
  - We want the interview to be at least one hour—no one can keep their guard completely up for one hour. This is how we can get comfortable and all learn more about each other for the purpose of the interview.
  - We want to encourage those conducting the interview to be willing to let their own guards down. Be honest about your experiences at Mytech, with your team, etc. This will both encourage the candidate to be open about his or her experiences as well as show a genuine participation and honesty in the process.

- **What to Look for in the Culture Interview**
  - Mytech Values
  - Humble, Hungry, and Smart Attributes
  - Make a Difference Training
  - Giver vs. Taker vs. Matcher
  - ABC Player (Culture vs. Performance Graph)

- **Intro Paragraph (What the Interview Is, What to Expect, etc.)**
  – Interviewee Facing Component
  - Was the culture interview explained to you? This is for us to get to know you and for you to get to know us. We spend more time together at Mytech than anywhere else. We are here for eight to nine hours a day with our peers, and it's important to have people on our team who know how to work together well. At the end of the day, the most important thing to us is that if a job is offered to you, you know what you're getting yourself into. Neither you nor we want you to get three months into the job and find out that this is not a fit. And that's why we encourage you to ask as many questions throughout this process and we will answer with honesty. We want to give you the best idea of what it's like to work here so that you can make the best decision if a job is offered to you.
  - This is just a template, a guide. It holds the information we want to cover before the questions, that's the important part. Otherwise, you can say it how you like.

- **Core Questions**
  - Core Questions that Culture Team member will be sure to touch on throughout the interview—based off of Humble, Hungry, and Smart.

Attributes

Humble

What was the most embarrassing moment in your career/biggest failure? How did you handle that embarrassment or failure?

- **Insight:** Look for whether the candidate celebrates that embarrassment or is mortified by it. Humble people generally aren't afraid to tell their unflattering stories because they're uncomfortable with being imperfect. Also, look for specifics and real references to the candidate's own culpability (The Ideal Team Player Interview Guide).

Can you tell me about someone who is better than you in an area that really matters to you?

- **Insight:** Look for the candidate to demonstrate a genuine appreciation for others who have more skill or talent. Humble people are comfortable with this. Ego-driven people often are not (The Ideal Team Player Interview Guide).

Hungry

What is the hardest you've ever worked on something in your life?

- **Insight:** Look for specific examples of real but joyful sacrifice. In other words, the candidate isn't complaining, but is grateful for the experience (The Ideal Team Player Interview Guide).

What do you like to do when you're not working?

- **Insight:** Look out for too many time-consuming hobbies that suggest that candidate sees the job as a means to do other things. That's not to say that there is one specific kind of activity that is an indicator of not being hungry. And it's certainly not to say that you're looking for someone who has no interests in life outside of work. But a long list of hobbies like extreme skiing, sled dog racing, storm chasing, and shark hunting might just be a red flag when it comes to someone who is not going to put the needs of the team ahead of personal pursuits (The Ideal Team Player Interview Guide).

Smart

How would you describe your personality?

- **Insight:** Look for how accurately the person describes what you are observing and how introspective he or she is. Smart people generally know themselves and find it interesting to talk about their behavioral strengths and weaknesses. People who seem stumped or surprised by this question might not be terribly smart when it comes to people (The Ideal Team Player Interview Guide).

What do you do that others in your personal life might find annoying?

- **Insight:** Everyone annoys someone, sometimes. Especially at home. Smart people are not immune to this. But neither are they in the dark about it. And they tend to moderate these behaviors at work.

Fun Interview Questions

- These are the questions that we most often used to ask and will continue to ask in the interview. We don't want the entire interview to be the Core questions, as those don't foster as much openness and comfortability. The 'Fun' questions will fill more of the time with chances to relax the room and allow for a more constructive, natural conversation.

- See attached document for list of questions open to all of the interviewers.

What is the Mytech Warriors Challenge?

- This is a one-year cultural initiative to create some fun and a little weirdness in the workplace. Mytech will be split into six different garrisons with about 16-17 warriors in each garrison, if we have full participation.
- Two challenges, a reward and immunity, will happen at each end of the month party. One challenge could be a little physical while the other will be more mental or puzzle like.
- Garrisons will split their warriors up at the beginning of each competition to determine who they want on the reward challenge and who they want on the immunity challenge.

Why Should I Participate?

- The Final Prize:
  - Win a $1,000.00 Best Buy gift card (one for each warrior in the garrison… yep I said for each).
  - Win a victory dinner at Fogo de Chão for the winning garrison.
  - Arrive to the dinner in style with a stretched limo from Mytech to the dinner and back.
- Help build the culture of teamwork and comradery in the workplace.
- Try to beat Nathan Abernathy at something, because he really wants to win the prize.

What If I Don't Want to Participate?

- We encourage as much participation as possible, but realize that these competitions will commence during non-business hours, and not everyone will choose to participate. If you choose not to compete for one reason or another, please turn your buff into a member of the culture committee before the February end of month party, so that garrisons can be rebalanced and to ensure your assigned garrison does not get penalized down the road from a warrior that is MIA (missing in action). Due to lots of moving parts and fairness to all participants, once you choose not to participate, that decision is final.

When Do We Compete?

- To ensure we are able to still provide the best IT experience for our customers, all warriors challenges will happen during non-business hours on the scheduled date of each end-of-month party. We will try our best to ensure that challenges don't exceed more than 15-20 minutes.
- Minnesota garrisons will compete at 5:15pm sharp CST
- Colorado garrisons will compete at 5:15pm sharp MST

Choosing a Garrison Leader:

- Every Garrison needs a leader, so the first task of each garrison is to nominate a leader of the garrison.
- The only caveat is that the garrison leader cannot currently be on the Mytech leadership team. The purpose of the leader is to provide one person that the culture committee can disseminate information to and get information from during the challenge.
- Leaders can change throughout the challenge, please just let the culture committee know.

MyTech Warrior Challenge - Rules of Engagement:

How Does My Garrison Win the Final Prize?

- If your garrison earns the most warrior battle axes throughout the competition, your garrison wins the final prize. If your garrison ties with other garrisons, a final challenge will ensue at the annual Mytech banquet to determine the winner of the Mytech Warriors Challenge!
- In order to be eligible for the final prize, you must participate in at least eight of the end-of-month parties. Exceptions can be made for this, please email culture@mytech.com if you have concerns about this.

How Do I Earn Warrior Battle Axes?

- Getting unsolicited customer feedback via email or carrier pigeon that aligns with our vision to provide the best IT experience in North America. Sorry CW surveys don't count.
- Only once a month if your garrison gets their warriors to engage in something outside of a scheduled Mytech function or Mytech warriors challenge event such as skiing, running, game night, happy hour, movie night. Take a group selfie and for each warrior in the photo they will earn a warriors battle axe for your garrison. Please note that the event needs to be at least an hour in length. Congregating in the parking lot after work for five minutes and calling it good won't count.
- Winning reward or immunity challenges.
- Other ways may be developed after the challenge starts, but will be announced to all before battle axes can be earned.
- Managers will or have provided a number/goal for you that will be determined at the end of each month. If you meet this number or goal, you will earn a warriors battle axe for your garrison.
- Please note some adjustments might be made if garrisons are not equally sized. We will ensure this is done as fairly as possible.

What Is a Reward Challenge?

- Your garrison will compete in a challenge for a monthly reward that is identified up front (i.e. happy-hour, gift-cards, lunches, group outings, advantage at next challenges).
- If your garrison is the only garrison that completes the challenge or completes the challenge the fastest then your garrison wins.

What Is an Immunity Challenge?

- Your garrison will complete in a challenge to win immunity. If your garrison wins then, they can't be afflicted at the next reward and immunity challenge.
- If your garrison is the only garrison that completes the challenge or completes the challenge the fastest, then your garrison wins.

Affliction:

- Affliction is designed to hinder a garrison during the next reward or immunity challenge.
- An affliction card will be drawn to determine what type of affliction will take place for the next challenge and if it effects a warrior(s) or the whole garrison. This will be determined during the garrison tribunal.
- Types of affliction could be; blinded eye (blind folding), muteness (can't speak) etc.

Garrison Tribunal:

- The heart behind the Mytech warriors challenge is for team building, so you won't be voting warriors out of your garrison, rather the garrison tribunal will determine what warrior(s) or garrison will be sentenced to afflictions during the next reward or immunity challenge.
- Each garrison will have their warriors name written onto a ribbon. If your garrison loses the immunity challenge then, all of your warriors' ribbons will be added to the basket for drawing.
- The first garrison that reaches five members or garrison colored ribbons drawn will be the losing garrison. If the affliction card identifies one to five warriors being afflicted and not the whole garrison then the warriors that will be afflicted will be based on the order they were drawn. If any of the blank ribbons are drawn due to warriors being MIA, the garrison that won immunity can choose who they want to be afflicted during the next challenge.
- If an afflicted warrior is not at the next challenge, the last garrison that earned immunity gets to choose the afflicted warrior(s) replacement at the time of the challenge.
- Since the CO and MN teams will be competing at separate times, the garrison tribunal will be filmed and uploaded to our Mytech YouTube channel and a link will be provided for all participants to view at their leisure.

SCOUT
TECHNOLOGY GUIDES

Scout Technology Guides

Scout Technology Guides exists to simplify lives. They love helping organizations design and implement technology that makes everyone more productive.

The company was founded in 2003 by Matt Dryfhout and two partners. From its inception, the partners wanted to build a unique company that would provide value to clients.

Matt views his role as Scout CEO as having three aspects: being an inspiring leader (to his team, vendors, and clients), assembling and developing the best team possible, and continually looking for ways to improve the company through networking with other leaders and studying and implementing best practices.

The desire to grow a company with an enduring influence in the Vancouver, BC community drives Matt in his leadership. He is grateful that his role with Scout allows him to touch lives on many different levels and help clients achieve their business goals.

Scout is a service organization, and in interactions with Matt and his team, it is quickly apparent that they take that very seriously. Their culture is built on these three pillars of servanthood: serving each other, serving our clients, and serving our community. It's how they live their purpose.

The Scout team has generously provided items that provide a look into their unique culture:

- Culture Journey

- Mission and Core Values

- Culture of Mentorship

Scout Technology Guides Culture Journey

By Matt Dryfhout

Initially the 'why' for starting my own business was pretty simple: it was the opportunity to become my own boss. I realized later that this was less about the opportunity at the time and more an inevitability as it is the way I'm wired. However, another characteristic to my wiring is always wanting to understand why things are the way they are.

Almost a decade later in 2013, I was sitting in the audience at Connectwise's annual partner conference, IT Nation Connect when Simon Sinek challenged us to figure out "Why do you get out bed every morning and why should anyone care?" This resonated deeply with me as 10 years into starting the company, I had no real answer to that challenge. This was the start of my culture journey.

Fast forward to today, 14 years in, I have bought out both business partners with whom I started the business. We have completely rebranded and built our culture with a purpose revolving around the statement 'Simplifying Lives.'

Early in the discovery of "Who are we?" and "What does it all mean?", our work in helping people with their technology and business challenges, attempting to simplify their lives was a recurring answer to Simon's question.

We further built out our values complementing our purpose and ended up with this:

We simplify lives.
Let's start with yours.
At Scout, we love helping organizations design and implement technology
that makes everyone more productive.

OUR CULTURE

Anchoring our purpose and three pillars of servanthood are our core values. Our core values are the fabric of our character. They are non-negotiable and influence every decision we make. Living and breathing our core values allows us to be the very best version of ourselves and when we are the very best version of ourselves, our team, clients, and community win.

SERVE - We take pride in serving our peers, clients, and community.

CONNECT - We build strong relationships with our clients and connect them with the right technology.

OWN - We take ownership and never give up!

UNDERSTAND - We work closely with you to understand your needs and meet them.

TRUST - You trust us to guide your business through what you will need in the coming weeks, months, and years.

SCOUT
TECHNOLOGY GUIDES

In order to reinforce that we actually care about these values, there is an open form for peers to submit examples they witness of peers exemplifying any one of our core values or purpose. I give out restaurant gift cards to each of the recipients at our monthly staff meetings where the submitter reads aloud their submission.

Another testament to our commitment to this (and trust in our team's integrity) is that there is no limit to the amount of cards I will hand out on a monthly basis.

In building a business that revolves around long-term relationships, with high emphasis on values and people, our single biggest strategy has been less about the E-Myth systems and process building and more about finding and acquiring the best fit people first.

Because of this people first strategy, we have exceptionally high retention and low turnover. For many years, we didn't have the credibility to make the claims we do today, but this summer I was so excited to celebrate Kris's 10 years, Marcel's eight years, and Paul's six years with us. See below a picture of our serve value wall in our office:

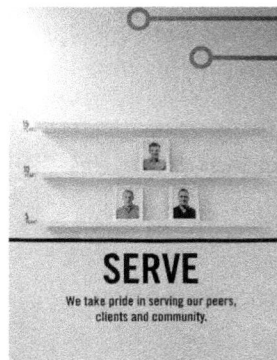

SERVE
We take pride in serving our peers, clients and community.

There is nothing I hate more than fake. If I make a statement about our company, we better be able to back it. Therefore, for many years, even though we knew we were building something special, I would stray away from commenting.

However, now that we have a track record and realize this is more than just a few lucky hires, we use it in every external touchpoint.

I'll list a few examples, starting with our office. We've branded our office with similar messaging as our webpage, but with the majority of it revolving around our purpose and values.

We make it a requirement when courting new prospect clients that our proposal presentation happens at our office, where we will have the chance to properly share who we are and what we're all about. If the prospect is not willing to invest the time to learn and connect with us in this way, it speaks to their level of commitment to the new relationship.

Secondly, our hiring process is unique in that we invite five to eight prospects to our office at once, and they interview together with a couple Scout folks. This allows us to efficiently meet a higher number of candidates than if we started with one on ones. Furthermore, it gives us the opportunity to share our culture with a great number of people in our community.

We send them off regardless of the outcome of the experience with a thank you gift for coming, and they leave with an impression that at Scout, something is different.

When developing our values I tried real hard to capture the collective answers of the whole team. But, as we moved further in to defining, this became harder. I generally don't like imposing my beliefs on others, this is what it felt like for me. However, I realized that this was actually my duty as the Founder and CEO: if not me, then who else?

Patrick Lencioni gives the same advice in his book *The Advantage*. The core values and purpose of the company not only need to be aligned with the leadership, they need to be exemplified.

This is the burden I proudly carry as I see it followed by our team of servant hearted people. When you get it right, this is not something that feels forced; it is who you are.

If you expose this to your prospective client and talent markets, it will attract people that share the same values. From what I have seen, this has been our recipe for success.

Culture of Mentorship

In a call with Matt, he shared how he has been considering business legacy topics such as exit and succession and has come to a unique conclusion: he is deliberately choosing not to select an exit date. He is committed and vested with his company.

The Scout leadership team desires that the company still be around in 100 years. Why 100? Matt said they chose that date because it is beyond everyone who is currently involved. It is a legacy number that will require them to build something that outlasts every person currently working as part of the Scout team.

To facilitate thinking through how people will transition out and how company value will pass from one generation to another, Matt has been working with his team around the idea of legacy.

In order to continue developing people, the team at Scout have developed a three-year vision and are using that to create individual career paths for employees. They have their current org chart structure and have designed an org chart for three years out.

They are putting employees in the chart in their current position and having conversations around their dreams for the future: "Here you are. Here's what we think the organization will look like in three years. Where do you want to be?"

As employees are identifying their desired future, Matt and his team are building a plan to get them to that new position. The Scout culture of mentorship involves casting vision for what is possible and then walking with people to transition from their current role to their desired career.

Scout is still early in developing this culture, but Matt's vision is working. People are staying and investing their lives as part of the Scout team. This year they were excited to celebrate key team members' 10-year, eight-year, and six-year anniversaries with the company.

The future is bright for Matt Dryfhout and his team as they work together to help everyone on their staff succeed, the staff that works at Scout today and laying the groundwork for the team to still be succeeding 100 years from now.

Week of _____

Big Rock #1

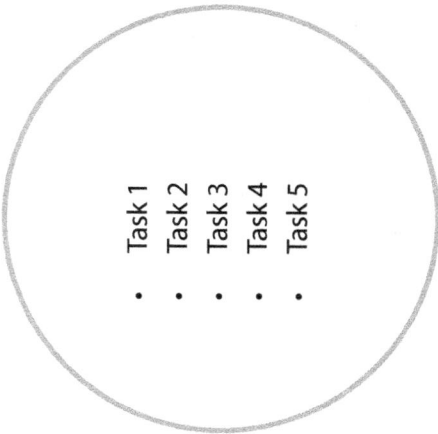

- Task 1
- Task 2
- Task 3
- Task 4
- Task 5

Big Rock #2

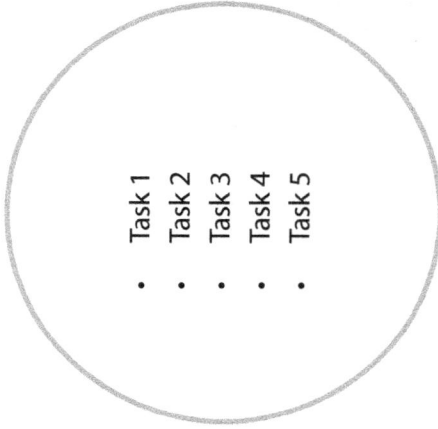

- Task 1
- Task 2
- Task 3
- Task 4
- Task 5

Big Rock #3

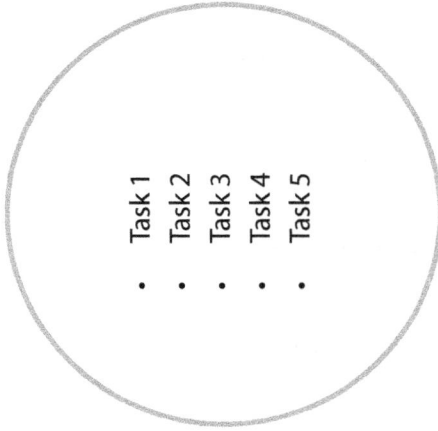

- Task 1
- Task 2
- Task 3
- Task 4
- Task 5

Monday

Tuesday

Wednesday

Thursday

Friday

If you make it a habit to spend five minutes filling out this sheet at the start of the day and spend five more minutes at the end of each day, you'll begin to see the benefit of your investment of time.

Jumpstart Your Day

1 - Start in Prayer.	Laurie starts her day with prayer to prepare her heart. She writes down requests or the names of people she is praying for. She often themes her days and will pray for HTG members one day, colleagues another, the leadership of her company the next, etc.
2 - Express Gratitude.	Write the names of 3 people you express gratitude to that morning. It can be sending a quick or text, writing a note, or making a phone call.
3 - Be Positive.	Write down a positive thought or quote for the day.
4 - Examine the Calendar.	Note any meetings or appointments.
5 - Review Priorities.	What 3 'big rocks' (priorities) are you committing to complete that day?

Powering Down Your Day

1 - Learning.	Record something you learned that day.
2 - Question.	Note something you are thinking about or a question you still need answered.
3 - To Do.	Record any lingering tasks to work on the next day or future actions you need to take.
4 - Determine Priorities.	What 3 'big rocks' (priorities) are you committing to complete the next day?
5 - Express Gratitude.	Record three things you are grateful for that day.

Jumpstart Your Day

✝	**1 - Start in Prayer.** Write down the names of people you are praying for or theme your days and pray for colleagues one day , the leadership of your company the next, etc.	
thankful grateful blessed	**2 - Express Gratitude.** Write the names of 3 people you express gratitude to that morning.	1. 2. 3.
☁	**3 - Be Positive.** Write down a positive thought or quote for the day.	
📅	**4 - Examine the Calendar.** Note any meetings or appointments.	
🪨	**5 - Review Priorities.** What 3 'big rocks' (priorities) are you committing to complete that day?	1. 2. 3.

Powering Down Your Day

💡	**1 - Learning.** Record something you learned that day.	
❓	**2 - Question.** Note something you are thinking about or a question you still need answered.	
➡	**3 - To Do.** Record any lingering tasks to work on the next day or future actions you need to take.	
🪨	**4 - Determine Priorities.** What 3 'big rocks' (priorities) are you committing to complete the next day?	1. 2. 3.
thankful grateful blessed	**5 - Express Gratitude.** Record three things you are grateful for that day.	1. 2. 3.

Company Communication Standards

What messages should we communicate and how should we go about communicating them to one another?

When Emailing:

- When you address an email that contains a request for action—only put ONE NAME in the 'TO:' box. When you put several names in the 'TO:' box no one is sure who should take responsibility, which leads to more emails.

- If you are in the 'TO:' box, think carefully before replying ALL to decide if everyone needs the answer. Do not move all names to the 'TO:' box when you reply.

- Put 'Approval' in the subject line when asking for a decision. Be sure to put a needed action item at the top of an email and use the remainder for the explanation. It is best to phrase the response in a simple yes/no format, so the approver can read your explanation and then reply to the suggested course of action listed at the top.

- If someone needs to be communicated information but doesn't need to act on it—put them in the 'CC:' box. Create a folder called CC and use a rule to move all emails with your name there to that folder to be reviewed less regularly because it does not require action. A daily review of the CC folder would be a good policy to set.

- Do not use the 'ALL' location lists to solicit donations for ANY cause. If you have a worthy cause for us to contribute to—use the newsletter to communicate that.

- Emails should be short and to the point. Make your point quickly and concisely. Type with clarity so your message is clear and easily understood.

- When someone sends a question to a distribution list through email, think twice before you REPLY ALL. Usually, only the person who asked the question needs the answer.

- On the subject of email subjects—do not send an email message without a subject. It makes them much more difficult to find in your inbox. Also, make the subject clear and informative about what you need and when.

- If you send someone an email request to do a task and they let you know that the task is complete in an email reply—it is not necessary to reply again with 'Thanks' or 'Thxs.' We believe that all of us know that the person who asked us to do the task is grateful that we got it done.

- Here are some reminders from the employee handbook related to email:

    o Remember that all email sent to/from your company address is company property

    o Do not use your company email address to conduct business for personal gain.

  o Never use company email for any illicit purposes including pornography, gambling, etc.

  o If you are away, be sure to turn on your Outlook "Out of Office."

- 48-hour response is required for all company email, 24 hours for those marked 'Approval.'

- Read and reread your email before you send it to avoid sending something that you will later regret.

- Check your email addresses to be sure they are going to the intended address.

When Talking with a Colleague Face-to-Face, by Instant Message, or on the Phone:

- Consider the personality and communication style of the person with whom you are interacting. The company has adopted the Make a Difference personality profiling tool. Use the insight provided by that tool to approach your colleague in a way that will make your communication most likely to be received well. Look for clues as to his/her personality 'animal' (this can be found displayed on their office door, a stuffed animal on their desk, a picture in their link profile, etc.).

  o **Lion:** Keep it short and simple. Be direct.

  o **Camel:** Provide detail and thoughtful analysis.

  o **Monkey:** Start with a joke or personal comment before focusing on the task at hand. Be relational.

  o **Turtle:** Begin a conversation slowly. Just sit together for a moment before you speak. Give them 'think time' before you expect a response.

- Slow down and take time to enjoy one another. Engage in a conversation 'give and take.' Share your ideas but listen, too.

- Be aware of your body language and tone. Are you open and inviting?

- Ask them if you are interrupting and if now is a good time for you to communicate. If it's not, ask to schedule a better time.

- When asking a colleague to collaborate on something with you, provide clear parameters of their role in the task and be upfront about different milestones and due dates involved with the project. Stay in close communication and provide frequent updates.

- End the conversation by asking, "Is there anything else I can do to help you?"

- Build trust and rapport by following through on the things you say you will do. If you know you are not going to meet a deadline, give your colleague as much advance notice as possible and come prepared with a proposed solution or new deadline.

Team Quarterly Communication

HUNDREDFOLD Harvest

Employee Name: _____   Manager: _____

Employee Position: _____   Manager's Title: _____

5 Question Clarity

1. What are we trying to accomplish?

2. Where do I fit in?

3. What are my boundaries and resources?

4. What's in it for me?

5. How am I doing?

Opportunities for Development

Goal Setting

Comments

Employee's Signature _____ Date: _____

Manager's Signature _____ Date: _____

HUNDREDFOLD Harvest

Four Stages of Learning

Introduction

There are four stages of learning. They are differentiated by a couple of factors: The level of competence of the individual and the level of passion or enthusiasm for the task.

STAGE	COMPETENCE	LEADERSHIP STYLE
Novice	*Unconscious Incompetence*	"I do. You watch."
Apprentice	*Conscious Incompetence*	"I do. You help."
Journeyman	*Conscious Competence*	"You do. I help."
Master	*Unconscious Competence*	"You do. I watch."

Coach's Questions

- To what extent am I prepared to alter my leadership style to be most effective for the person I am trying to help? Ask yourself the hard question: Which is more important—maintaining my comfort in my leadership style or developing the potential of my protégé?

- Am I really prepared to let someone make a mistake in order to speed the learning process?

One Last Tip From Coach

If there's not a little bit of anxiety around the decision to give them more... if you're completely certain they'll be successful, you've waited too long. Don't wait too long! You'll lose the enthusiam, energy, and excitement that help them learn a new role.

Challenge

Identify a situation and use this tool to help you develop one person on your team in a specific way. You are never going to get anywhere unless you start. So pick someone or a skill to teach and take them through the phases.

Resource Library

We encourage you not to plan in isolation. Use this book to work on your individual plans but engage corporately with colleagues and reach out and collaborate with others who can offer valuable feedback on your plans and challenge your assumptions.

We have created and will be adding to an online Resource Library full of tools such as templates, coaching articles, videos, etc. You can find it at hundredfold-harvest.com/resources.

We will continuously be adding to and growing this library, so if you have developed a tool that you think might be of help to others, please let us know! Also, if there are certain tools you would find useful, let us know and we will see what we can do to accommodate you.